Charles
BRONSON

Charles
BRONSON

David Downing

St. Martin's Press
New York

Printed in the United Kingdom.

LIBRARY OF CONGRESS CATALOG CARD NUMBER: 83-060715

ISBN 0-312-13010-4

First published in Great Britain by W. H. Allen & Co. Ltd.

First U.S. edition

10 9 8 7 6 5 4 3 2 1

CONTENTS

Part One

COAL MINER'S SON

Ehrenfeld

> I've loved all my children, six sons of mine
> I pray that they never must work in the mine
> For the Black Lung will get them, they'll die just like me
> Hang the lantern in the window, give my love to Marie
>
> (from 'Give My Love to Marie' by James Talley)

IN THE DECADES spanning the end of the last century ship after ship steamed into Upper New York bay, tied up at the wharves of Ellis Island, and discharged its human cargo. Thousand upon thousand of emigrants from eastern and central Europe clambered out of the holds, eager for their first sight of the Land of Opportunity.

Perhaps they caught a glimpse of the Statue of Liberty, half a mile to the south across the bay, as they were herded into the waiting area popularly known as 'The Stockyards'. Some were met by earlier arrivals, some spoke enough English to be let loose on the new country. But for the rest liberty was something still to be earned.

One such newcomer, a strong young Russian from Lithuania, bore the surname Bunchinsky and a Christian name which the officials either disliked or found impossible to spell. They re-christened him Walter, and told him to wait with the rest of the non-English speakers. Eventually someone decided his future by placing a tag around his neck marked 'coal mines'. Soon he and similarly tagged individuals and families were shunted into box-cars on one of the waiting trains. A day or so later they found themselves deposited in a small Pennsylvania coal town called Ehrenfeld.

'Town' was something of a misnomer. Ehrenfeld was a mine, not a town, a company fief, not a public place of dwelling. The workers worked in the company shafts, spent their wages in the company store, slept in the company houses. These, though cold and damp and devoid of plumbing, were unlikely to collapse, which was more than could be said for the tunnels beneath the earth. Mining at this time was a hard and risky business. Machinery was minimal, and the company didn't want to spend its profits on safety measures. Cave-ins were common, and if they didn't get you, disease probably would.

Walter Bunchinsky was a digger, a face-worker. Like his co-workers he was paid by the ton, not the hour, and the tons required to sustain a living meant a life spent either working or sleeping. Sixteen hours a day and more they hacked at the coal, ears tensed for the sound of a cave-in, breathing in the black dust which ate their lungs away. There was no hope of escape, because all they could earn went to pay off the debts accummulated at the company store, the rent due on the company home. If any miner managed to dig so much coal that saving became possible, then the company laid him off. If anyone talked of unions, then being laid off was the least of his worries. To live in Ehrenfeld was to live in a cage.

Still, there he was, in the Land of Opportunity, and though it must soon have become crystal-clear that he would never live to sample its fabled delights, the hope remained that his descendants would reap such benefits from his sacrifice. Bunchinsky married an American-born Slav, Mary Valinsky, and they began to build a family, to create an oasis of hope and care in lives scarred by industrial slavery.

The first child, a daughter, was born mute, and two of the sons would enter the world physically-handicapped, one a hunchback, one with a heart condition. Two other children died in infancy. But the Bunchinskys were also blessed, if such a word makes sense in such a context, with ten healthy children. Their fifth son, Charles Dennis Bunchinsky, was one of these; he was born on 3 November 1921.

'Charlie', as he was known from the cradle on, was the apple of the family's eye. It was now understood that more than Walter's sacrifice would be needed; the elder sons too would have to work down the mine. But Charlie was the hope for the future; he would be educated while the others worked, he would inherit the opportunity to escape the company's grasp.

Apple or no apple, the future Charles Bronson

was not to enjoy a carefree childhood. He hardly ever saw his father, in later years remembering only that 'we always addressed him through our mother. He didn't like the noise after a shift in the mine. . .' The ever-present trials of poverty left an indelible mark. 'Milk was only a nickel, but we couldn't afford it. When my baby sister was born, Mom fed her mostly warm tea instead. She didn't have a baby bottle, so she used an empty ketchup bottle and stuck a nipple on it.'

In recent years the Bronson publicity machine has churned out stories of the star's youth—of losing his virginity at the age of five, of being 'sold' by his mother for one summer's work on a farm, of fights and burglary and nights in jail. Most of these stories seem exaggerated, and few of them, as Steven Whitney has pointed out in his biography of Bronson, tie in with those facts which are established. For example, Bronson reportedly stated that there 'was no love in my home. I was one of fifteen children and the only physical contact I had with my mother was when she took me between her knees to pull the lice out of my hair.' But others who lived in Ehrenfeld at the time saw things differently, and remember a much-respected and loving woman, and a child who was always the family favourite.

But, exaggeration or not, it hardly seems to matter. Perhaps Bronson's later embellishments, if that's what they were, represented nothing more than a heartfelt need to communicate to people who could not begin to imagine what life was like in a place like Ehrenfeld, the horrors and degradations of his early years. He certainly found out young what suffering was. Like the rest of the family he listened to his father coughing his life away in the back room. 'At the end, he was choking on every breath, and we all pretended we didn't hear anything. How do you explain what that does to you? You never forget that.'

Death was a regular visitor in the Bunchinsky household. The two brothers to whom Charlie was closest, George the hunchback and Tony with the weak heart, soon followed their father to the grave. Each of these deaths, which occurred when Charlie was in his early teens, hit him hard, and he reportedly became more withdrawn, more angry with a world so devoid of compassion. This, according to one of his accounts, was the reason his mother packed him off for that summer to a farm in upper New York state. 'I was thirteen years old and getting into all kinds of trouble. I was wilful and rebellious, and my mother was afraid I'd turn bad.'

America was now scraping along the bottom of the Great Depression, and families like the Buchinskys—they had dropped the 'n'—had to run faster to stay in one place. The older brothers were now working double-shifts in the mine, and Charlie, though still at school, could not escape forever. In 1937, at the age of sixteen, he started doing a night-shift, whilst continuing to attend school by day.

He graduated in the summer of 1939, and began looking for a job in the world above-ground. But the World War had not yet begun the task of resurrecting the American economy, and there were none to be had. He had no choice but to go down the pit. 'We were so much in hock to the company store that I'd work sixteen-hour shifts, day after day, and at the end of the month, by the time we'd paid our debts, I'd have maybe a dollar to spend.' It seemed as if the family's hopes for his future had come to nothing; the cage had claimed him too, education or no education. 'The worst thing of all was the frustration, the feeling that you were trapped, and that that was all life would ever have to offer. I can remember being down the mine, hacking away at the goddam coal and weeping at the sheer hopelessness of everything.'

A wider world

FOR ONE PERSON at least the war was to prove a blessing. Early in 1943 Charlie Buchinsky was drafted into the US Army and out of Ehrenfeld. At the age of twenty-two he began to discover the fabled world beyond the mines.

He had no complaints, in fact quite the reverse. 'I never had it so good,' he admitted later. 'Men were complaining all around me. But I was eating and sleeping well, and I thought "Jeez, this is great!"' Of course, his lack of experience of the outside world was painfully, and embarrassingly, noticeable. 'You come out of a coal mine town and you're frightened. You even have to ask how to tie your tie . . . I guess I had a chip on my shoulder for a while. I got into fights. But in time, I found I could be as good as anyone else.'

The war still had more than two years to run. Buchinsky drove a mess truck around Arizona for a few months, and was then posted to the Pacific theatre as a B-29 tail-gunner. He flew around twenty-five missions, and collected one bullet-scar in a shoulder. In February 1946 he was given an honourable discharge.

He returned to the family in Ehrenfeld, but only to the family; the mine would never claim him again. Ex-GIs were given time and money to re-adjust, and Buchinsky made full use of the breathing-space. He took some aptitude tests arranged by the Veterans Administration, and came up with a strong leaning towards art, a moderate inclination towards journalism, and an apparent suitability for social work. Any of them seemed a better bet than digging coal.

At the end of 1946 he moved to Philadelphia—he didn't have the money to reach New York—and enrolled at the Hussein School of Art. His fees were paid courtesy of the GI Bill, his living-expenses catered for by a succession of part-time jobs. In the little spare time that remained Buchinsky patronised the local gym, and there he got friendly with several members of the local Plays and Players theatre group, who invited him to exercise his artistic skills on their scenic back-drops. To everyone's surprise, not least Buchinsky's, he soon found that acting was a more satisfying business than painting, at least insofar as earning a future living was concerned. And, to add further spice to this new life, he fell in love with another group member, Harriet Tendler.

The Plays and Players group didn't put on any productions in the summer months, and many of its members spent the seasonal break in the nearby coastal resorts, earning the following winter's food and rent. In 1947 Buchinsky rented deck-chairs on the Atlantic City boardwalk, before graduating to a permanent post with the Thrill-O game on Hamid's Amusement Pier. His co-worker there was Jackklugman, later known for many films and the TV serial *Quincy*.

After another winter in Philadelphia, and another summer in Atlantic City, the two men decided to try their luck in richer pastures; they rented a room in New York City and hawked around for stage parts. Buchinsky got two minor roles in productions of *The Night of January 16th* and *The Stevedores*, useful experience but hardly the grand entrée to the theatrical big-time. When their money ran out, he and Klugman delivered mail, and come summer they were back on Hamid's Pier calling out the lucky numbers.

The season of 1949 ended somewhat prematurely, and in dramatic fashion, with the burning down of Hamid's Pier. This occurrence, though doubtless distressing to Hamid, seems to have forced some decisive action out of Buchinsky. On 30 September 1949 he married Harriet, and together they set off for the promised state of California, carrying with them five suitcases ('Four and a half of them hers'), one umbrella and around $250. Hollywood, as everyone knew, was where the dreams came true.

Heavier than thou

BUCHINSKY ENROLLED AT an acting school, the famous Pasadena Playhouse; they had agreed that Harriet should be the bread-winner until such time as Charlie had made it as a professional actor. At this stage he harboured few illusions as to his career potential. 'I went to the Pasadena Playhouse to study speech just to improve my diction. I knew I was going to do character parts. I was already identified as a character by my ridiculous speech. At that time, all the leading men were Cary Grant types. They all looked like the guy who got the girl. I didn't look or sound like the guy who got the girl.'

He was an enthusiastic student. 'By the time I got to California,' he later recalled, 'I had become too involved in acting. It was my entire life. I had no part of any other society. I ate and breathed it. It is really dangerous that way.' But dangerous or not, it got him noticed. When one of the Playhouse instructors heard that director Henry Hathaway was looking for a rough-hewn young man for a minor role in his next movie, he

18

suggested the dedicated young Buchinsky. After less than a year in Hollywood, the coal miner's son had broken into movies.

The film was U.S.S. Teakettle, later re-named You're In The Navy Now. It was one of those semi-comic melodramas full of physical fun and apple-pie morality which spread like a disease through the post-war world, with Gary Cooper playing the all-too-familiar fresh-faced young captain licking his ship and crew into some sort of all-American shape. Buchinsky played one of the frolicsome sailors, handy enough with his fists to be sponsored for an inter-ship boxing tournament. The role, though small, did run throughout the movie; Buchinsky had not done badly for a first time out. Lee Marvin, who also made his debut in the film, had an altogether more nondescript part.

Unfortunately, the film was not well received by the public—hence the re-naming—and Buchinsky's next few parts would represent something of a step backwards in screen-time terms. On the Teakettle set he had met agent Gus Trembling, one of the many specialisers in extra and bit-part work who handled enought actors to make 10 per cent of not much seem like a living wage. Trembling agreed to represent Buchinsky, and quickly found him two small roles in two reasonable films, The People Against O'Hara, a Spencer Tracy vehicle directed by John Sturges, and The Mob, a marginally better-than-average crime drama. This was hardly progress with a capital P, but sharing a scene with Tracy, then considered the paradigm of Hollywood quality acting, was not an experience to be lightly dismissed.

More minor roles followed, in the firefighting drama *Red Skies of Montana*, the semi-documentary prison drama *My Six Convicts*, and the romantic soap opera *The Marrying Kind*. But though the parts were small—in the last-named film almost to the point of invisibility—Buchinsky was gaining invaluable experience, leaving a good impression and, most important of all, making useful contacts. In his first year as a movie-actor he had worked with Hathaway, Sturges and Cukor, three of Hollywood's top directors, and he had gotten to know many of the leading and up-and-coming actors. When jobs were available in the future there would be many people around who could vouch for him.

According to Whitney, 'the attitude with which Buchinsky approached each new job helped him win many of these small parts. From what can be remembered by his early co-workers, Charlie was always very professional. Knowing his parts were small and basically expendable, he did exactly what the director wanted. He was always on time, and he always knew his lines.' Perhaps this was Ehrenfeld speaking—places like that were not noted for engendering a blasé attitude towards job security. Or perhaps Buchinsky was just naturally reliable. Either way, directors noticed. When Cukor needed an actor for a minor role in the classic Tracy-Hepburn film *Pat and Mike*, when Hathaway needed someone for

20

the Tyrone Power vehicle *Diplomatic Courier*, they asked for Buchinsky. Dependability was a saleable commodity in Hollywood, and after only two years in the business, Buchinsky seemed to be carving out a secure niche for himself.

It was a humble niche, though, and Buchinsky was already itching to take another step up the ladder. The trouble with Gus Trembling, from his clients' point of view, was that he didn't seem to share their ambitions. When he got Buchinsky two more small parts, this time in films— *Bloodhounds of Broadway* and *The Clown*—which lacked any distinction, the actor decided to dispense with his services.

This was a risky move to make—actors without studio contracts needed agents—but it also proved either astute, fortuitous, or both. Buchinsky, it turned out, had already done enough to impress Meyer Mishkin, an altogether more prestigious agent. Mishkin handled only stars and high-class supporting actors, and he believed that Buchinsky could, in time, join the latter category. Fewer-but-better film parts and a lot of TV exposure would do the trick.

This estimation of Buchinsky's eventual niche, as a high-class character actor filling in the spaces left by the stars, was also shared by the actor himself. With his face and voice he was doomed to play 'mostly punks, construction workers, punchy fighters, all the parts nobody could play because of their educational backgrounds. I could play them because I was just a bum. Most actors are impersonators but in me they got the

21

real thing. I came along when you had to look a part to play in it.' This was OK, it was the way things were; what Buchinsky aspired to was the chance to play the main punk, the one who came third or fourth on the cast list behind Romeo and Juliet.

Mishkin's TV blitz strategy didn't work out too well; he got Buchinsky only one part, in *The Doctors* series. So it was back to movies, eight of them in 1953-4. The first was *House of Wax*, a good horror movie starring the youngish Vincent Price as a leering nasty who liked adding human corpses to his wax collection. Buchinsky played the mad assistant Igor, all twitches and shuffles and demonic mumbles. It was a memorable role, well encapsulated by the publicity still showing Buchinsky's head amidst a row of wax busts.

Director André de Toth was clearly satisfied, using Buchinsky twice more in the ensuing year, as an incompetent nasty in *Riding Shotgun*, one of the many off-beat Randolph Scott westerns, and as a convict in the gangster drama *Crime Wave (The City is Dark)*. Neither film had much to recommend it, but at least Buchinsky's name was creeping up the credits, to sixth position in each case. As part of their publicity campaign for *Crime Wave*, Warner Brothers actually released a summary of Buchinsky's film career. It was definitely progress.

Better was to come. The episode of *The Doctors* in which Buchinsky had appeared had been directed by Robert Aldrich, and the two men had got on well together. When the new Lancaster-

22

Hecht production company chose Aldrich to direct their first movie, *Apache*, Buchinsky was given a good part. And when the same team made *Vera Cruz* later in the year he was cast again. Both films were to be tremendously successful.

Apache starred Burt Lancaster as an Apache warrior who refuses to be exiled in Florida with the rest of the tribe's defeated fighters. Escaping from the train carrying him East, he manages to get back to home territory, and retires to the mountains with his bride (Jean Peters). Eventually convinced that a one-man war will achieve nothing, he abandons the warrior role for that of the farmer. The whites of course won't let him be, and in the end a warrior's death is forced upon him.

As a treatment of the Indian theme *Apache* was ahead of its (Hollywood) time. Despite this, and despite the fact that Lancaster and Peters were less than convincing members of the Apache nation, the film proved both powerful and popular, something of a rare combination in the early 1950s. Buchinsky was fourth on the cast list—his best yet—but this ranking was somewhat flattering, in that Lancaster, with or without Peters, took up about 98 per cent of the screen-time. Buchinsky, as Hondo the Indian scout, had about six scenes and six lines. Yet he was notice-able; he had the right brooding presence, he looked the part. Seventeen years later he would play the Lancaster role in a very similar picture and show just how it should be done.

Vera Cruz also starred Lancaster, this time

teamed with Gary Cooper, in search of Mexican/ French loot circa 1867. Cooper played the upright southern gentleman who needs money to restore his civil war-ruined estates, Lancaster an altogether less scrupulous character who grins like a shark and double-crosses at the drop of a stetson. The plot revolved around the reluctant partnership's attempt to escort, and eventually hijack, a gold convoy en route to Vera Cruz.

Buchinsky played Pittsburgh, one of Lancaster's unshaven cut-throat companions. Unlike Hondo, whose rare excursions into speech were for lines like 'she'll be a widow soon', delivered with appropriate deadpan menace, Pittsburgh was the garrulous sort, whose idea of fun was pulling women to the ground and play-fully announcing that he liked it 'when they scream'. It was a much more nondescript part, and the film itself, though a big hit in 1954, has not withstood the test of time quite as well as *Apache*. Lancaster's performance now seems too exaggerated, Cooper's too predictable.

But *Vera Cruz* did offer one harbinger of the future. Pittsburgh was prone to playing the har-monica, something which Buchinsky would do to greater effect fifteen years later, in the film which turned him almost overnight into a superstar.

A third western, *Drum Beat*, was of more immediate significance. It was the first time he used the name Bronson—with the Hounds of McCarthyville skulking round Hollywood Slavic names didn't seem so fashionable. More impor-tant, it was the first film which he managed to 'steal' from the nominal star, no less a personage than Alan Ladd, one year after *Shane*.

The director was Delmer Daves, a much underrated talent with a string of excellent westerns to his credit, *Drum Beat* not least among them. The newly christened Bronson played Captain Jack, the leader of a renegade Indian group, and though the actor only figured sixth on the cast list, the role was central to the film. Captain Jack had some memorable lines to deliver, most notably his tart rejoinder to the local priest: 'If paradise is so great, then you take my place'.

The excellence of the role brought out the excellence of the actor. The *Los Angeles Times* reviewer pronounced him 'only slightly less than sensational ... it is he that dominates the picture'.

With such a success under his belt Bronson must have looked forward to a rise in the quality of the films and parts he was offered. But, not for the last time, such expectations were to be disappointed. He appeared in another crime drama, *Big House U.S.A.*, which though reasonably well-made proved none too popular at the box-office. After that, nothing.

Mishkin reverted to Plan A, this time with more success. Through 1955-7 Bronson appeared in more than twenty TV shows, ranging from the common-or-garden series like *Gunsmoke, Medic* and *Have Gun, Will Travel* to the more prestigious 'Theatre' presentations and one of the earliest 'TV movies', *Explosion*. These parts were

25

invariably larger than those he had been playing in movies, and his face and talents were receiving a wide airing.

There was also cause for domestic rejoicing, for on 27 February 1955 Harriet gave birth to their first child, daughter Suzanne. The family had just moved out of their last apartment and into their first house. For a man with memories like his, Bronson was now making a lot of money.

But despite the film successes and the TV successes the right sort of film offers still failed to materialise with any sort of regularity. Certainly a film like *Target Zero* was unlikely to advance anyone's career. Bronson received third billing in this Korean War-based action romp, his highest yet, but the film was distinctly third-rate, and the cast's commitment to it was not helped by the tragic death of two explosive experts on-set.

The next movie was a distinct improvement. Delmer Daves had been hired to direct *Jubal*, a much-postponed 'adult western' project ('adult' being short for adulterous), and he cast Bronson as the title character's best friend. Despite the shock-horror tag *Jubal* turned out to be a fine western, with notable performances by Glenn Ford and Rod Steiger in the two leading roles. Bronson was also noticed, the *Hollywood Reporter* describing his performance as 'outstanding without over-emphasis'.

But once again success proved no more than its own reward. He was offered roles, lots of them, but none which seemed anything more than what had gone before: more punks and construction workers and scowling Indians with a dozen lines and a few assorted grimaces. Bronson could play such parts in his sleep by this time, and he refused to cooperate in the digging of his own rut. Perhaps the birth of a child had increased his sense of responsibility, sharpened his ambition, perhaps he had just decided that it was time to make a stand. He was thirty-five now, and with each year passing his chance of stardom was diminishing. He turned down all the offers and switched agents, leaving Meyer Mishkin for Lester Salkow. It might not help, but it could hardly hurt him.

Salkow got him a part in yet another western, *Run of the Arrow*. He was back in loincloth for this one, playing Blue Buffalo, a 'sympathetic Indian' (in the 1950s, one who got on with white men). The film, though commercially unsuccessful in America, has since acquired the status of a minor classic, largely on the strength of director Sam Fuller's European reputation. But such accolades didn't help Bronson in 1956. His part was disappointing, lacking the resonance of a Captain Jack, or even a Hondo. And what was probably more galling still was that Rod Steiger—not an actor of the Cary Grant school—had starred in both his most recent pictures. If someone with Steiger's face could make it right to the top, then why not Bronson? He seemed to be facing an invisible wall to further progress. If he couldn't break through it, then he'd have to find a way around it.

Smaller ponds

SOMETIME IN 1957 Bronson and Salkow decided on a change of tactics. Instead of attempting the transition from 'A' movie support to 'A' movie star, they would attempt the transition from 'B' movie star to 'A' movie star. At a lower level Bronson would prove he could carry a movie on his own. He agreed to take the lead role in two Gene Fowler Jr 'B' films, *Gang War* and *Showdown at Boot Hill*, and to do a lot more TV work.

Both the films were interesting. Fowler was no hack, and he recognised in Bronson the potential for playing tough guys that went beyond the stereotype. In *Gang War* he played a high school teacher who chances to witness a gangland slaying. His initial reaction is to steer clear of involvement, but the police persuade him to testify and, as a result, his wife is brutally murdered. He sets out to avenge her, despite police discouragement, and eventually confronts the gangster leader responsible. But the latter is dementedly weeping, his empire already overthrown by rivals, and Bronson's character realises that fate has done his work for him.

He's a tough character all right, but not so 'tough' that he doesn't break down in tears when his wife is killed, not so devoid of feeling that the gangster leader's fate leaves him totally unmoved. It was a new, more rounded hero-figure for Bronson, and a precursor of much that was to follow. The plot of *Gang War* also presaged much of the plot of *Death Wish*, the film that was to make him a superstar in America, some sixteen years later.

Showdown at Boot Hill was also a reasonably subtle example of its genre, with Bronson cast as a US Marshal of less than perfect ethics, who kills a wanted man in cold blood, and happily visits his victim's town to pick up the promised bounty. Unfortunately his victim was popular, and the townspeople refuse to identify his body. Again a tough character is rendered more complex by a situation which transcends stereotype; again he finds that his 'toughness' offers no solutions to the problems confronting him. Sheltered from the townspeople's wrath by a hotel waitress, he gradually comes to accept his guilt and the need to atone for it.

The third starring role was not so auspicious. *When Hell Broke Loose* was one of those movies which had everyone the poorer for its making. Bronson played a reluctant World War Two con-script who manages, between outbursts of sadly choreographed violence, to fall in love with a fraulein (with a heart of gold) and to foil a plot to assassinate General Eisenhower. The script, like the title, seems to have been written by a wooden computer.

The fourth and last of these 'B movie' starring roles offered a complete contrast. *Machine Gun Kelly* was directed by innovator-on-a-shoestring Roger Corman with real flair. Bronson played the title-role, a gangster who is both repellent and pathetic, whose total lack of feeling for his victims' lives is 'balanced' by a morbid fear of his own death, a total emotional subservience to women, and a near-pathological prudery. A real 1950s American hero.

The film begins with a bank robbery, all effectively violent, and some neat gangster movie lines like: 'You know, kitten, I'm gonna get you a nice little white mouse to play with'. But the hero's tough exterior soon bursts open to reveal a heart of pure jelly. He is petrified by a caged mountain lion, and goes to pieces during a second robbery after catching sight of a coffin. At the end of the. film, surrounded by cops, he refuses to go out in the traditional blaze of bullets and glory. 'I didn't want to be Public Enemy No. 1' he mutters pitifully, and when asked by the constabulary why he didn't shoot it out, he replies, ''Cos I knew you'd kill me'. The cops look suitably chagrined at having been denied the excuse.

In America the film was released as the bottom half of a double-bill with *The Bonnie Parker Story*, and though generously received by the critics was unable to transcend its humble presentation. In Europe though, and particularly in France, critical acclaim and public enthusiasm went hand in hand, and *Machine Gun Kelly* was a minor sensation. European audiences had long accepted an American superiority in the making of 'action' films, and had learnt to live with the inevitable Disneyland theology which permeated them. But *Machine Gun Kelly* was different—it seemed, to some, to combine Hollywood's talent for 'action' with a sense of moral realism more typical of the French 'new wave'. Whatever its place in cinematic history, the film was a good one by any standards, with central performances by Bronson and Susan Cabot which did it ample justice. In the former's later heyday in Europe, *Machine Gun Kelly* would be often and enthusiastically revived.

Unfortunately, the stimulation of Parisian film-goers was not one of Bronson's prime career aims, and the relative success of this short stint as a 'B' movie star was not noticeably advancing those aims. It was also becoming apparent that 'B' movies were in any case a dying industry. Challenged by TV, the cinema moguls were beginning to realise that movies would have to offer something special, that they would have to outspend their TV brethren on sets and stars and locations. There would be no money left for making 'B' movies, and no need to make them anyway. Western and gangster 'quickies' could be done just as easily by TV, and the punter wouldn't have to queue in the rain or pay cash for his or her dose of escapist garbage.

Bronson's agent started getting him more work on TV. It paid well, and it helped to establish his

31

face with the growing American audience. It also offered, in general, a greater variety of roles, more opportunities to prove his talent as an actor. Of course, many of these roles were ersatz 'B' movie roles, guesting as the villain whom the series hero would knock off that week. Thus he made appearances in *Sugarfoot, Have Gun, Will Travel*, Lee Marvin's *M Squad*. Occasionally he would play the sick man whom the series hero would cure that week, as in shows like *Medic* and the later *Doctor Kildare*. But between such routine assignments there was the occasional challenging part, in the one-off plays put out in series like *Alcoa Premiere* and *Playhouse 90*. Here he was given the opportunity to act, to prove himself more than a heavy of uncertain extraction. And there was always the possibility of a series to himself, and the chance to kill or cure his own guest stars.

Sometime in 1957-8 Four Star/Desilu producer Don Sharpe, together with partner Warren Lewis, acquired the rights to the biography of a well-known police photographer, Mike Kovacs. They had a movie in mind, but this fell through, and a TV series seemed a good alternative. Sharpe had admired Bronson's TV work and wanted him for the part—*Man With A Camera* was born. Each week Bronson would find himself involved in a variation of the Hollywood plot with a different cast of Hollywood characters.

So much for art. *Man With A Camera* was sponsored by General Electric as a showcase for, believe it or not, a particular type of flash-bulb. According to Bronson 'it was the biggest "plug"

32

show in the history of television ... I was the hero, a news cameraman, but the director had to keep stopping the action to make sure the label on the equipment was visible. By the tenth week I realised I was playing second banana to a flash-bulb'.

But successfully. After one fifteen-episode series had been completed, the show was still popular enough for a second batch of episodes to be made, and fourteen more were planned for 1959. Eleven had been made when disaster struck in the shape of Polaroid, who introduced a revolutionary new flash bulb onto the market. General Electric's model, and *Man With A Camera*, were suddenly obsolete. The sponsors duly pulled the plug.

It was, perhaps, a blessing in disguise for Bronson. Twenty-six episodes had established his face without forever typecasting him as tough-guy photographer. More important, those episodes had shown him to be more than capable of holding an audience in an unambiguously 'good guy' role. This, when taken together with his 'B' movie roles and long hitch playing background heavies and morose Indians, showed him to have a considerable acting range. He was undoubtedly a star now, if only of the second league variety. He would not lack for work, and he could, to a large extent, afford to pick and choose his roles, both on TV and in films. After almost ten years as a professional actor it was not such a bad place to be.

PART TWO

KEEP
A'KNOCKIN', BUT...

O'Reilly

DURING HIS TIME With A Camera, Bronson had appeared in two more 'A' movies, *Ten North Frederick* and *Never So Few*. His part in the former, a weepie with pretensions and little else, wasn't big enough for an extra—he had presumably found himself on friend Gary Cooper's set when someone was needed to cover one of the floor-marks. The latter film, set in Burma during the Second World War, featured Sinatra and Lollobrigida up to their palm-fronds in one of those torrid tropical romances which punctuated Hollywood's war. There was also a hefty ration of anti-oriental action, including one massacre of prisoners by Sinatra and Co. which looked forward to the good old days of Vietnam. Bronson's character was involved in the action rather than the romance, and in this department he, like everyone else, was upstaged by newcomer Steve McQueen.

Still, appearing in this particular debacle turned out to have its compensations. It re-introduced Bronson to director John Sturges, whose next movie was to boost the cinematic careers of just about all those involved. With most of its plot and much of its characterisation lifted from Kurosawa's classic *Seven Samurai, The Magnificent Seven* was to prove one of the most popular westerns ever made.

The casting of such a film was obviously crucial. The 'seven' had to be seven recognisable individuals, each with a well-defined 'character', for the movie to succeed. Yul Brynner was chosen to lead the band of soon-to-be-obsolete gunfighters reduced to defending a Mexican village for a living; Steve McQueen, after his triumph in *Never So Few*, was a natural choice for hero no. 2. For the rest, Sturges banked on up-and-coming, rather than established, stars: James Coburn, Robert Vaughn, Horst Buchholz, Brad Dexter and Bronson. And of those five, only Dexter, who played the most stereotyped role, was not to go on to bigger and better things.

Bronson's O'Reilly was cast in the mould he was making his own. He is first seen chopping wood, swinging his axe like some great Polack Goliath. His words are clipped, his eyes hooded, his desire to communicate with the rest of the human species about as developed as Papua New Guinea. Yet as the film progresses he emerges as by far the most sympathetic of the seven. They are all cut off from normal life, from families and homes, but he is the one who loves children, who feels his exile most keenly. It is too late now for a change of course; instead he lectures the worshipful village children, telling them that it is their peasant fathers, working the fields from dawn to dusk, who really deserve their respect. Predictably, he is killed trying to pull one of the children out of the line of fire. But predictable or not, it is still the film's one genuinely moving moment, and superbly played by Bronson. A flash of real feeling is rare enough in commercial melodrama, and this one leaps out of *The Magnificent Seven*, rivalling in impact the film's other great scene, the more conventional but beautifully-staged knife-versus-gun-fight which sent James Coburn's movie career into orbit.

Bronson's scene should have done as much for him, but it didn't. He picked up his biggest cheque to date—$50,000—a figure which reflected both his new TV fame and the substantial clout wielded by his new agents at MCA. He was picked out for fulsome praise in most reviews. But none of it turned the essential trick. He went back to working in TV, went back to (admittedly bigger) supporting roles in mundane 'A' movies. He must have wondered what he had to do to break through. If O'Reilly couldn't make him a star then what level of success or excellence could?

Compensation could still be found at home. The marriage remained unusually happy by Hollywood standards, and the couple's first son was born in February 1961. In any case, Bronson was not the sort of man to expect anything to come easy. He carried on painting in his spare time, visions of his childhood, the mining towns wreathed in coal-dust and despair. One day, perhaps, he would reach the top of the slag-heap called Hollywood.

Supporting actor first class

IF HE DID attain new heights, it would be more down to luck than judgment. Bronson's inability to tell good parts from bad continued to be his undoing. *The Magnificent Seven*, the TV work, the 'B' movie star roles—they had all enabled him to display the range and depth of his talent, had provided him with the opportunity which he now proceeded to squander, making awful movie after awful movie.

His first post-*Seven* film was *Master of the World*, a sort of Jules Verne composite, with Vincent Price as the mad scientist intent on making everyone else see reason. He builds a gigantic flying fortress called the 'Albatross', takes to the air with the usual mixed crew, and starts dropping bombs on anyone who refuses to disarm. Bronson is the good-guy government agent intent on spiking his guns, whenever the heroine will allow him the time. The usual clichés emerge, hover, and fall flat. Needless to say the mad scientist disappears beneath the waves just as the popcorn runs out. The world has been made safe for rearmament once more.

Bronson got some good reviews—'a likeable hero' someone called him—but the film went down with the 'Albatross'. He went straight into *A Thunder of Drums*, a John Ford-style cavalry drama which badly needed John Ford. The Indians practised smoke-signalling and minor massacres while old, grizzled, harsh-with-a-heart-of-gold Richard Boone tried to lick young, arrogant, upstart-puppy-with-a-heart-of-gold George Hamilton into shape. Bronson's soldier drooled with lust whenever Luana Patten walked by, and indulged in high-pitched cackling whenever anything else happened. Which wasn't often. It was an abysmal film, and an appalling part.

Things didn't improve much in 1961. He made *X-15* with director Richard Donner, playing one of three astronauts piloting America's first rocket-ship. Someone must have been doing his or her homework, for once again the film's only moving scene involved Bronson in conversation with a child. The other 104 minutes were over-technical and lifeless. The film flopped.

Kid Galahad, by contrast, was a big success, thanks to the drones of Elvis Presley fans who hadn't yet realised that his movies had degenerated along with his music. Again Bronson had the most sympathetic role, as the star's self-sacrificing trainer. For a Presley vehicle the dialogue was surprisingly good, and the supporting actors, who included Lola Albright and Gig Young in addition to Bronson, had some fun delivering it. But the songs and the plot were indifferent, Presley was Presley, and the 1937 original was never in danger of being emulated. Bronson himself said: 'I went to see it with my wife, and it was so bad that we left in a hurry, while it was still being shown'.

Between making films, he was also doing a lot of TV work, guesting in the odd series, acting in the odd one-off drama. He appeared in the pilot premiere of a new series, *Empire* (*Big G* in Britain), and proved so popular that he became a semi-regular. Richard Egan played the ranch patriarch, newcomer Ryan O'Neal the romantic interest. In Britain the first episode was given a cinema release as *This Rugged Land*.

The great success continued to elude Bronson. He was now passing forty, and few people in his profession climbed much higher after reaching that age. Perhaps John Sturges' new movie, *The Great Escape*, kindled some hope in Bronson's breast, but if so he was doomed to disappointment. There was nothing wrong with his character, a claustrophobic tunneller; it was both sympathetic and real, which was more than could be said for Richard Attenborough's super-teutonic British mastermind, or Steve McQueen's hollow Biggles-on-a-motorbike American. There wasn't much wrong with the film from a commercial point of view, and it was a huge success. But from Bronson's point of view it might just as well have been a failure, for all the mark it left on his career.

Making it though did leave a profound mark

on his life. One of the British actors given a major role was David McCallum, and the two men, both inveterate loners in a gregarious trade, soon struck up a firm friendship. When McCallum's wife, ex-actress Jill Ireland, suffered a miscarriage, both men spent much of their off-set time visiting her in the Munich hospital. She found Bronson quite different from what she'd expected. 'Before we'd met, all he'd been to me was a face on the screen and a rather intimidating one at that. But suddenly, close up, I saw in this man such unbelievable tenderness, such depth of feeling for my plight.' The three of them became very close, a situation which Bronson presumably found both warming and emotionally confusing.

He returned to the States to make another indifferent movie, *Four for Texas*. This was a 'Clan' romp, with Sinatra and Dean Martin proving how irresistibly sexy they were to Ursula Andress, Anita Ekberg and the audience. Bronson played an energetic villain. The film must have made a lot of schoolboys laugh, and provided them with material for some esoteric fantasies. Otherwise it seemed to serve no purpose save the making of money, and it didn't make much of that.

Bronson was now losing his agents—MCA were withdrawing from that sphere of activity. He must, in any case, have been wondering by this time just what they were for. But he was used to having one and at this moment the McCallums arrived in Hollywood with David's agent, Paul Kohner, in tow. He agreed to handle Bronson; they have been together ever since.

Kohner's arrival did not, however, prevent Bronson from making 'The Great Mistake'. At some point in 1964 he turned down the starring role in an Italian-made western entitled *A Fistful of Dollars*. 'It was just about the worst script I'd ever seen,' he said later. 'What I didn't realise was that the script didn't make any difference—it was the way Leone was going to direct it that would make the difference.' Clint Eastwood seems to have been more attuned to the possibilities inherent in the script, but then he didn't have so much to lose as Bronson.

The size of the error would take time to become apparent. Meanwhile Bronson's marriage was slowly falling apart, and he took himself off to Germany once more to appear in *The Battle of the Bulge*, a Hollywood rendering of the 1944 Ardennes offensive. Compared to most such offerings, this was a surprisingly good war film, with an outstanding performance by the late Robert Shaw in the role of a panzer general addicted to military combat. Bronson was his reliable self as the tough American soldier, sharing one scene with Henry Fonda and one with Shaw. It was the sort of role he did so well, and the sort he wanted out of.

Back in the States he landed another semi-regular spot in a TV series, this one based on the best-selling western novel, *The Travels of Jamie McPheeters*. It was the usual hokum, and it spawned the usual movie spin-off, *Guns of Diablo*. But Bronson obviously preferred the devil he knew, because Leone's unusual hokum still held

45

no attractions for him. He turned down the Lee Van Cleef role in *For A Few Dollars More*. 'This time I said it was just like the first movie... It was, but what I didn't understand was that everybody wanted it to be just like the first movie.'

This was only half the story. Bronson, and, for that matter, most of the American film industry, had no understanding of what made the 'spaghetti westerns' so popular. It was not merely, as most of Hollywood condescendingly believed, that Italians, being excitable people, liked lots of violence. They, and others, liked believable moral codes, believable settings, stylish violence, and characters endowed with a mythic, almost religious, quality. The traditional Hollywood western was woefully deficient on all counts; its format remained firmly rooted in the pre-war years.

Far from coming to grips with Leone's 'neo-realism', Hollywood was still trying to catch up with the realism of 1950s European cinema. Real people in real settings facing real situations was something of a challenge to the dream factory, and its managers' answer was to put Elizabeth Taylor and Richard Burton in front of Big Sur and have them talk earnestly about freedom while the servants prepared the meals. *The Sandpiper* must rank as one of the worst movies ever made, and Bronson's acceptance of the major supporting role served only to confirm his brilliant knack for picking the wrong projects at the wrong time. He played an aging beatnik sculptor, busy sculpting a nude Liz Taylor while she and Burton got on with the 'adult love story'. The dialogue was indescribable, but Bronson blamed director Vincent Minelli. He was 'very Hollywood, not very modern. He is also inflexible, and if you have suggestions to offer, he's afraid to take them into consideration. . .' It is difficult, though, to imagine what suggestions, short of dynamite, could have saved *The Sandpiper*.

At home, his marriage to Harriet continued to deteriorate, and late in 1964 the couple separated. Bronson now spent most of his leisure time with the McCallums. David had become a teenage idol almost overnight as the Russian moppet in *The Man from UNCLE* TV series, but his marriage to Jill was also showing signs of stress.

Bronson took himself off to Louisiana to make *This Property is Condemned*, as first support to Natalie Wood and rising star Robert Redford. He had high hopes for this one. 'I've been offered a part in a picture which is entirely different from any I have ever done,' he told an interviewer. 'It will be so different that it could change my whole career. . . In the picture, I sell myself as a sexy kind of individual. Which is a little different. Everything else I have ever done has been hard, rough and rugged, and has had nothing to do with women.'

It's hard to see how he could have been so hopeful. He had about eight scenes to play in the film, and only one of them extended much beyond the minute barrier. In his first appearance he slaps Kate Reid's behind, in the second he tries to seduce daughter Alva. In the third he sits mute in the railway workshop. And so on. The opportunities for acting were minimal, the role almost contemptuously small. Bronson blamed director Sydney Pollack for not enlarging his part, but the film only really made sense as the story of two people. Natalie Wood looked alternately gorgeous and despairing, Robert Redford acted out the Prince Charming-with-flaws role he went on to make his own in the 1970s, and Bronson simply disappeared.

So, far from changing his whole career, *This Property is Condemned* served only to emphasise his status as a supporting actor, a crutch for the stars to walk with, and over. Stardom, now so close, must have seemed further away than ever.

Unshaven lone rangers

THE SANDPIPER NOTWITHSTANDING, Hollywood was inching its way along the road towards greater realism in films. It would be gratifying to report that 'truth', or some such shining light, guided the moguls on this perilous journey into uncharted territory, but, a few individuals excepted, this was not the case. As usual the guiding star in question was nothing more than the strong smell of money.

Reality, or at least some vague notion of it, was one of those things which the cinema could offer in its life-and-death struggle with TV. And, as the 1960s progressed, it became clear that mankind could bear more of the stuff. Not only was youth becoming increasingly disenchanted with the way the society operated, but—and this was the crucial point—cinema audiences were getting younger. Like the record companies, the cinema industry was slow to catch the spirit of the times, but once they had caught it, they began the task of turning it into hard cash with enormous enthusiasm.

How were films to be made more realistic, and how were heroes to be constructed in this new age? First off, the traditional Cary Grant-type figures, wearing inner haloes and looking like they'd just got back from the manicurist, were out as far as serious movies were concerned. The stereotype no longer had any social impact, any ability to stir audiences. It was relegated to the realm of the comedy-thriller.

Second, there had to be more explicit, and simply more, sex and violence. For the next decade, lady heroines were out. Women, toppled from their romantic pedestal, were required to be witches, bitches or whores. They didn't have to always take their clothes off, but they did have to always look like they might. This wasn't very realistic, but then film-makers were not the only people in the late 1960s to confuse real with explicit.

As for violence, it did get more real. The Lone Ranger's bloodless victims turned into people bleeding like geysers on full power. War was shown to be hell, not merely announced as such. The only thing missing was any sense of responsibility.

Thirdly, the middle class was out. It had been eaten up by its soap opera image, and any attempt to take a long, hard and commercial look at the suburban world was out of the question. It would be more than ten years before movies like *Ordinary People* took the first hesitant steps in this direction; for the moment all eyes were focused on those above and those below, the corruption

50

of wealth and the corruption of poverty.

All this 'realism' left its mark on the new hero. As he wandered from bloodbath to bed and back again his character took shape. There was no time for the manicurist, not much for shaving; survival was too time-consuming a business. Corruption stared this hero in the face wherever he looked, so illusions were only there for the shedding. Bitterness or anger was one norm, a stoic acceptance of man's imperfection the other. Either way, there were no answers. This hero lived for the moment.

A new generation of leading men arrived to play him: Lee Marvin, Clint Eastwood, Donald Sutherland, Jack Nicholson and many others. They played similar parts in similar movies. The new hero was obviously anti-establishment—a rogue cop, an outlaw or criminal, a rebellious soldier. He was also stylish, had to be, because only style could mask his essential impotence as an anti-establishment force. But like all heroes he was effective in man-to-man combat, whether physical or cerebral.

What he didn't have to be was either pretty or charmingly witty. Which obviously suited Bronson, who was neither, at least on the screen. When Lee Marvin picked up the 1965 Oscar for a particularly un-Cary Grant-like performance in *Cat Ballou*, Bronson must have realised that the times were changing. Hollywood's move towards 'realism' wouldn't make him a superstar, but it would remove one barrier to progress in that direction. The bandwagon was now running his way, and all he needed was some good parts, a fair slice of luck, and the sense to jump aboard.

The last lap

IN 1966 DIRECTOR Robert Aldrich was putting together a 'realistic' war movie. The script for *The Dirty Dozen* already had a long history, having passed through at least six typewriters, and the casting was also giving Aldrich some headaches. The studio wanted John Wayne to lead, but the director didn't want to make *that* sort of movie, and hung out for Lee Marvin. The studio only relented once Marvin had proved his box-office drawing power by taking the Oscar.

Filling out the dozen presented Aldrich with the sort of problem Sturges had confronted in casting his seven, and not surprisingly the ever-reliable Bronson was one of those enlisted. He might have expected to be making the same sort of film, and at one level he was, playing one member of a group reluctantly conscripted to take on the forces of evil. But the differences were more striking. The seven were all good guys who happened to be gunslingers at a time when gun-slinging was going out of fashion. They therefore deserved both admiration and sympathy. The dozen were all convicted murderers and rapists, offered a last chance of salvation on a suicide mission behind enemy lines. Their only claim to sympathy was their anti-establishment attitude, which in itself rested on rather dubious moral foundations.

The Dirty Dozen can also be usefully compared with *The Battle of the Bulge*. The latter was a thoroughly traditional war film, replete with conventional attitudes, full of purely physical violence. In its depiction of the Second World War it was undoubtedly more true to military reality (if not human reality) than was *The Dirty Dozen*. The Ardennes Offensive, though compressed in space, time and tanks, was faithfully recreated, and the salient historical points all rendered more or less accurately.

The plot-line of *The Dirty Dozen* was, by contrast, absolutely ludicrous. The idea that a vital military target could have been entrusted to a gang of convicted prisoners defied any notion of realism. Yet, and it was a big 'yet', the characters in the later film *seemed* more real, the violence *felt* more real, the dialogue didn't sound like it had been written by hired hacks (even if it had). Because there were no clearly defined good guys the film lacked the usual numbing predictability. And the level and intensity of the violence, both physical and emotional, was enough, in 1967, to keep anyone awake.

Of course, it was all something of a con. As Stephen Farber put it: 'The movie has it both ways; we are asked to identify with the scrappy

54

underdogs and cheer when they make fun of their superior officers, but we are never asked to endorse any genuinely unconventional behaviour ... the film never questions the military ethos or the validity of war, it only taunts certain details of the establishment'. An anti-establishment audience could cheer them on as renegades, a pro-establishment audience could admire them as effective, no-nonsense warriors. Both could be stimulated by the violence with a clear conscience. What, after all, was wrong with burning German officers, women and servants alive in a cellar? War justifies everything, either because it's necessary (the establishment view) or because it stinks (the anti-establishment view). The film itself was careful not to make distinctions; it concentrated on simply piling up the corpses.

Bronson, predictably enough, was not in tune with this new world. '*The Dirty Dozen*,' he said, 'was nothing more than a diversion.' It was also, in his opinion, much too violent.

Such films rarely do much for the careers of the actors involved. In *The Dirty Dozen* they were called upon to maintain an air of sullen defiance, to speak, usually sarcastically, in monosyllables, and to give the general impression that they had just crawled out of a gutter. Each man was given a quirk rather than a character. It was the film which reflected the times, the actors were just there to make the film work.

The contrast with Leone's westerns was significant. Eastwood shot to fame not because the dollar films reflected the times (although they did), but because his character seemed equipped to survive those times. He had an air of detachment; he was above it all. He seemed in control. The dozen clearly weren't above anything; they could hardly control themselves, let alone their environment.

Bronson was still a supporting actor because he had not yet found a role, or more important still, a series of overlapping roles, which allowed him to embody the yearnings of the audience. Eastwood exemplified control through the intelligent use of violence, Wayne the traditional male, Newman the embittered survivor, Brando the crucified saint. Bronson was . . . an actor. A good one, indeed, but only an actor. It was moving to watch a tunneller struggle with his claustrophobia, to see a gunfighter trying to impart wisdom to worshipful children, to feel Kelly's morbid fears—they were all roles that could be related to. But that was the problem. It was the roles, and not *a* role, which was being presented to the cinema audience. Bronson stood for no set of attitudes, represented no potent myth in the public mind of how things were or how they could be. He had no 'persona' which tied all the characters together, so that they reinforced each other, expanded each other.

Fortunately, the vagaries of circumstance were pushing him slowly in the right direction. Returning to America he found no suitable roles available in American films, and reluctantly turned to the European-produced variety. He refused to work in the European cinema *per se*, still regarding this as a step backwards, but he agreed to star with Anthony Quinn in a European-financed western, *Guns for San Sebastian*.

It was a disaster. He played an Indian once more, this time ranged against a fake priest and his village flock. The script was bad, Quinn over-acted, and only the Morricone score made the film vaguely bearable. According to Bronson, 'it was one of the worst films I ever made. But I got on well with (director) Henri Verneuil. The failure of the film wasn't his fault. The screenplay was very difficult; there were six screenplay writers, all with different ideas, and, with Anthony Quinn, they were responsible. . .'

Undeterred he went into another Mexican western, *Villa Rides*, behind a hairy Yul Brynner and an apparently sleeping Robert Mitchum. Again the script was a disaster, with pseudo-philosophical chat about the horrors of war san-dwiched between incoherent bloodbaths, but this time Bronson had a good part, as Villa's blood-thirsty henchman Fierro. One reviewer thought the role sadistic, but Bronson's performance, full of nice touches, managed to suggest a character very much torn between the demands of war and the stirrings of compassion hidden deep within his soul. He handled the humorous scenes with great panache, more or less saving the movie in the process from the performances of its two 'stars'. It was a fitting end to his career as a supporting actor.

Part Three

AN ANCIENT RACE

Breakthrough

IN THE 1950S the revitalised European and Japanese film industries had turned out many a movie worthy of respect. But—and it was a big but—such respect was rarely accompanied by big money. Such films, beyond the land of their birth, played in capital art-houses, won awards at the burgeoning festivals, were analysed in esoteric magazines. But they offered no threat to Hollywood's dominance of the huge English-speaking mass market for entertainment.

When a challenge to this dominance did appear, in the mid to late 1960s, the American film industry, so used to considering TV as its main competitor, failed to take it seriously. Leone's 'Dollar Trilogy' reaped spectacular commercial success almost everywhere, and Hollywood was more than willing to ape its superficial attractions, but generally speaking the view of foreign films as either art, beneath contempt or both remained fundamentally unshaken.

Bronson was someone who shared these views.

As a first generation immigrant he was in some ways more American than the founding fathers, as a Hollywood actor who had come to prominence in the 1950s he seems to have taken American dominance of the world's commercial cinema for granted. When he was offered, while shooting *Villa Rides* in Spain, a part in an Anglo-French co-production his initial reaction was to ignore it.

Fortunately for him, agent Paul Kohner was more in tune with the times. He tells the story: 'In 1968 Alain Delon was looking around for someone to play his tough American soldier-of-fortune partner in a British-French co-production called *Adieu l'Ami*. As an actor, he had studied Bronson's work in pictures like *Machine Gun Kelly*, and liked it. The next thing that happened was that Delon's producer, Serge Silberman, showed up in Spain. Silberman pitched Bronson on the fact that in the American film industry, all the money, all the publicity goes to the pretty-boy types. In Europe, he told him, the public is attracted by character, not face. . . Bronson always had resisted doing European films before. . . This time he was only half convinced by Silberman's arguments, but I made a deal for him to do *Adieu l'Ami*.' Apparently Jill Ireland helped Kohner and Silberman to push Bronson in this new direction.

The star, in his own words, was 'getting the message'. And while he was shooting *Adieu l'Ami* Bronson got another offer he was wise enough to accept. Having rejected Sergio Leone twice out of

62

hand, having then turned down the 'Ugly' role in the third 'dollar' film because of prior commitments to *The Dirty Dozen*, Bronson now accepted the Eastwood-type role in the Italian director's fourth and most ambitious western, *Once Upon A Time in the West*. At last, after years of disastrous choices, he had picked out two winners in a row. And two was to be enough.

Adieu l'Ami, a stylish thriller set around the uneasy partnership of two heroic rogues (Delon and Bronson), opened in Paris early in the summer of 1968 to mixed reviews and an anything-but-mixed public reaction. In a fourteen-week premiere engagement the movie was seen by half a million people, and all the house attendance records were comprehensively shattered. It was the sensation of the year in France, and Bronson suddenly found himself sharing a pedestal with the likes of Jean Gabin, Jean-Paul Belmondo and Delon.

Once Upon A Time in the West soon turned *Adieu l'Ami* into a minor triumph. Its premiere engagement in Paris was to run for nearly two years, pulling in more than a million viewers. And despite the presence of Henry Fonda (an old French favourite), Claudia Cardinale and Jason Robards, it was clearly Bronson's film. He had found—stumbled on might be more accurate—the persona which gave him a special appeal, and almost overnight he had become one of Europe's top stars.

It was a different world. All the frustrations of the last ten years melted away. In October

Bronson and Jill Ireland were married, closing the book on the long and unsatisfactory hiatus which had begun in Munich five years before. Only real stardom in America continued to elude him. *Adieu l'Ami*, which suffered from bad distribution and some appalling dubbing, sunk without trace; *Once Upon A Time in the West* was given a few derisory cinema bookings and then quickly sold off to TV.

But the American industry was beginning to take notice, and to amend its view of Bronson as the perennial second or third support. Scripts and starring roles came pouring through the letter-box of his new thirty-three room Bel Air mansion and, true to form, Bronson picked out one of the least suitable. *Twinky* (sometimes known as *Lola*) was an older-man-meets-nymphet love story, a sort of expurgated *Lolita* set amidst the totem poles of the swinging sixties. Bronson's reason for taking the part (the older man, not the nymphet) was that he 'was a little tired of falling off horses, or rolling down stairs, or having hot ashes thrown over me'. He played the part well, and some reviews were more than generous, but it was not the kind of role he needed to maintain the new momentum.

Fortunately, such a role was now offered and accepted. René Clement, a French director with an international reputation, needed an American actor for the lead role in *Passager de la Pluie (Rider on the Rain)*. He liked Bronson's performance in *Adieu l'Ami*, and Alain Delon helped to convince him that Bronson would be perfect in the new

Previous page: The still from *Chato's Land,* which made
  Bronson's name

Top: Bronson in his first film, *You're in the Navy Now,* 1951

Above: Bronson, Claudia Cardinale and Jason Robards during
  the making of *Once Upon A Time in the West,* 1968
  (KEYSTONE PRESS AGENCY)

Opposite page: Filming *Twinky* on Chelsea Embankment with
  Susan George, 1969 (KEYSTONE PRESS AGENCY)

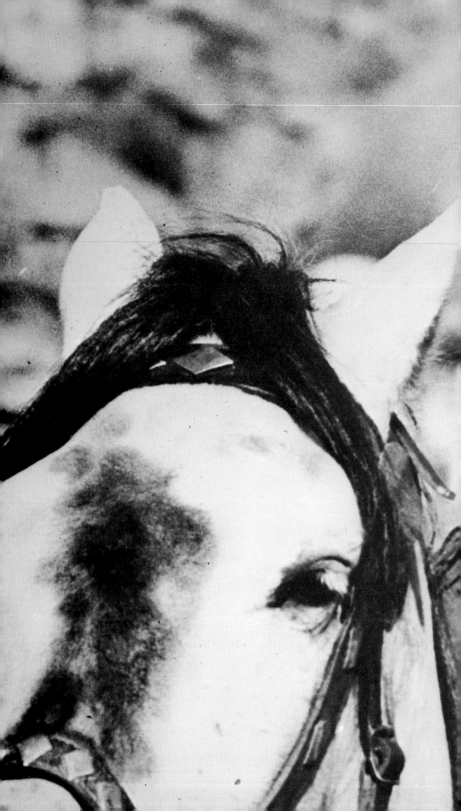

Previous page: Bronson as Link in *Red Sun,* 1971 (KEYSTONE
PRESS AGENCY)

Above: Bronson and his wife Jill Ireland celebrating the opening
of *Cold Sweat* with the director Terence Young and his wife
(KEYSTONE PRESS AGENCY)

Above: The Mechanic in action
(KEYSTONE PRESS AGENCY)

Left: A scene from *Breakout,* 1975

Following page. Top: Death Hunt in which Bronson starred with Lee Marvin

Following page. Bottom: Filming on location near the Mexican border for *Borderline,* 1980
(KEYSTONE PRESS AGENCY)

film. Their confidence was to be fully justified. Bronson's performance proved to be so powerful that the film's credit cards were changed to give him higher billing than his female co-star Marlene Joubert. In France the movie was an instant and enormous success.

According to Bronson, *Passager de la Pluie*, was 'the real beginning for me'. It was the first huge success he had not needed to share with other male stars. The film's popularity was his popularity, and he was now the biggest star on the continent. Old movies like *The Magnificent Seven, Machine Gun Kelly, The Great Escape* and *The Dirty Dozen* were re-released, each with credits re-arranged to give Bronson top billing. Old TV episodes were tied together into movies just to cash in on his new popularity. He had finally reached, in Europe at least, the top of the glittering pile. And he had done so with three excellent films, three excellent performances, and an appeal to audiences which he alone could make.

'Harmonica' and cousins

A STATION IN the middle of nowhere—echoes of *For A Few Dollars More*. Three men arrive, lock the station-keeper in his safe, and settle down to wait for the expected train. They don't look like simple fare-dodgers.

For something like ten minutes they, and the audience, wait. The windmill creaks, drops of water fall from the tank, a fly buzzes around. One of the men (Jack Elam—the face of a thousand westerns) pulls out his gun and traps the fly in its barrel. Then the insect's whine is absorbed by the whistle of the approaching train. Fly and audience are released.

The three men prepare themselves, standing in the traditional gundown line, facing the halted train. But no one appears to get off. The train begins to pull out, and suddenly the music of a harmonica becomes audible above its retreating roar. As the last coach clears the station a man is revealed on the far side of the track. It is Bronson. One minute invisible, the next filling the screen. A brief sneering conversation ensues, and we find out that the threesome are acting on orders from 'Frank'. Then the guns boom, all four fall, and only Bronson gets back up again.

The plot of *Once Upon A Time in the West*, though somewhat hard to follow in the cut version still shown in most cinemas, is not particularly complicated. The arrival of 'Harmonica' (he has no other name), with obvious intentions on the life of Frank (Henry Fonda), merely throws one more spanner into an already complicated works. Frank is a professional heavy hired by railroad baron Morton (Gabriele Ferzetti) to clear the designated route of recalcitrant land-owners, and in the second sequence of the film he and his gang are seen mowing down one such family, the McBains, who happen to control the only source of water for miles around.

What Norton and Frank don't know is that McBain has got married, and while her husband is being slaughtered bride Jill (Claudia Cardinale), an ex-New Orleans whore, is arriving at the local railhead in time to inherit the land and the problem. Finding McBain dead, and unaware of the land's importance to the railroad, she decides to return to New Orleans. But a friendly, enigmatic outlaw, Cheyenne (Jason Robards), and the mysterious stranger with the harmonica both prevail on her, none too gently, to stay. Cheyenne's reasons remain obscure—he just likes her, perhaps—but 'Harmonica' is clearly intent on frustrating Frank.

Morton now begins to see Frank as a hindrance rather than a help, and tries to buy off his gang.

frank kills him, and then rides out to the McBain ranch to find out why 'Harmonica' has been obstructing him. In the ensuing gundown he is mortally wounded, and on the 'point of dying' is given his explanation. 'Harmonica' then rides off with Cheyenne, leaving Jill to act as an 'earth mother' to the railroad workers.

It is not an exceptional plot, but it is an exceptional film, for two main reasons. One is the richness of detail, the almost zen-like clarity applied to every scene and shot. The opening sequence is typical of the rest, apparently empty of action, but in fact crammed with the 'reality' which most movies cannot reach. In this respect *Once Upon A Time in the West* can only be compared with Stanley Kubrick's *2001: A Space Odyssey*, and in other ways the films seem almost like mirror-images of each other. The spaceships become locomotives, the solar system the boundless frontier, and Kubrick's traveller into the future becomes Leone's Man of the Past.

But whereas Kubrick's film only operated at the two timeless levels, the magic of the commonplace and the magic of the all-embracing vision, Leone manages to fill the space between with characterisations which, though hardly profound in an emotional sense, are nevertheless redolent with a sense of history, of a particular time and space.

The five principal characters can each be measured against several yardsticks. The most obvious, and the most traditional, of these is the ethical. Morton and Frank are the 'bad guys'; Jill,

Cheyenne and 'Harmonica' are more noticeably blessed with the milk of human kindness. But of the five only Frank could be said to approach the level of stereotype, and even his murderous greed is to some extent explained, if not actually excused. Morton is an evil capitalist straight from the mould, prepared to hire the likes of Frank to get his dirty work done, but there is at least some sense in which his ends begin to justify his means. The fact that he is a cripple—a state of being usually reserved for sympathetic characters—further enhances the ambiguity of his 'appeal' to the audience.

On the 'good' side there is no one garbed in spotless white. Cheyenne is an outlaw, with many a dastardly deed to his name; Jill is an ex-whore who prefers ransacking her deceased husband's house to the more tedious business of mourning him. 'Harmonica' has no compunction about endangering her life in pursuit of his vendetta against Frank. Against this, Cheyenne is prepared to help Jill without demanding the traditional reward, and she means no harm to anyone. The reason for 'Harmonica's' obsession with revenge, as eventually revealed in one of the most striking flashbacks ever put on film, seems strong enough to justify all his actions.

Seen in terms of 'purpose', only Cheyenne of the five seems content with things as they are. The other four are all driven by something—Morton by his trans-oceanic vision, Frank by his greed, Jill by her desire to 'do something' with her life, 'Harmonica' by his thirst for vengeance. Each of these purposes ties the character into—or, in 'Harmonica's' case, out of—the fabric of history. Morton and Jill are the two faces of the West's future; he represents the necessary destruction which the civilising process will wreak, she the community which will eventually spring up on the ruins of the old frontier society. The other three all represent the past, and are defined by their reaction to the looming future. Cheyenne recognises and accepts the passing of the old ways. He will not change, but neither will he seek to reverse the flow. Frank also recognises it, but he is torn between acceptance and rejection. He tries to topple Morton and take his place, and so secure himself a niche in that future. But he also rides to meet 'Harmonica', admitting the difference between himself and his erstwhile boss—'It wouldn't have bothered Morton to know you were around somewhere.'

Most of the time 'Harmonica' has no need to consider 'history'. His quest has put him outside normal time and space. 'I don't invest in land,' he says at one point, as if to confirm his distance from the society around him. In a sense he could well be dead, just as the avenging US Marshal in Eastwood's *High Plains Drifter* turns out to be the avenging spirit of a dead US Marshal. Cheyenne confirms this in a way, telling Jill that people like 'Harmonica' 'have something inside, something to do with death.'

But when Frank arrives from the gundown 'Harmonica' identifies himself with the other. 'Just a man,' Frank describes himself, and

'Harmonica' murmurs 'an ancient race' in reply, adding, as the camera watches the railroad, that 'other Mortons'll be along and they'll kill it off'. Both men belong to that ancient and doomed race—individuals who deal with other individuals as individuals. They are untrammelled, untamed, free in the way that animals are free, both savage and innocent. Frank is killed and 'Harmonica' rides off, leaving Jill and the future behind.

To sum up, the character of 'Harmonica' personified the free man (untamed, unbound by society), the purposeful man (even though the motivation remained undisclosed to the end of the film), the effective man (fastest with the gun, quickest with the brain), and the 'good' man. In 1969 this was a potent composite. Though the great clashes of 1968 were over, the dust was far from settled. For an audience, a mostly young audience, which tended to view society as unfree and life as apparently purposeless, what better hero could have been devised? He was as effective and as 'good' as John Wayne, as purposeful as Che Guevara, as free as a riot. To a society with no apparent future, he offered a vision of paradise in the past.

Personas are more than characters, but 'Harmonica' offered Bronson a model for the persona he needed. And, as fortune would have it, the parts of Franz Propp and Dobbs in *Adieu l'Ami* and *Passager de la Pluie* were remarkably similar, almost variations on the same theme. In all three films he had played strangers bursting into

71

existing situations, with past unexplained and purpose undisclosed, with kindness in his heart and death in his hands. And because all three films were so successful, and the parts all so similar, something called 'Bronson', some image that was quintessentially his, grew to be bigger than the films themselves. He had finally become more than an actor, more even than a star. He was a figment of the world's imagination, a dream of how things might have been or how they still could be.

Momentum (and not much else)

WITH THIS NEW level of success Bronson's personal style changed somewhat. He became no more gregarious, but the trappings of superstardom were certainly not hidden away. He now travelled from set to set with wife, children (when not in school), and an entourage big enough to fill a medium-sized hotel. Some observers put this new flamboyance down to Jill Ireland's reported love of the good life, others thought it was simply Bronson's way of enjoying the rewards of the long struggle. What else had it all been for?

After completing *Passager de la Pluie* Bronson and entourage took off for Turkey, where he was due to co-star with Tony Curtis in a 'rip-roaring adventure tale', *You Can't Win'em All*. This was *Vera Cruz* revisited, with Turkey circa 1922 standing in for Mexico circa 1867, and both stars playing the Burt Lancaster role. The idea was reasonable enough, the execution left a lot to be desired. Such films need strong characters (though not necessarily real ones), imaginative violence and witty dialogue. *You Can't Win'em All* had indistinguishable characters, routine violence and a script for morons. The director, Peter Collinson, showed no aptitude for softening the blow.

Still, the film scored well with European audiences, presumably on the strength of Bronson's new popularity. His next movie, *Citta Violenta* (later released as both *Violent City* and *The Family*), took the Bronsons back to America with an Italian director, Serge Sollima. Jill Ireland played female lead to her husband's male lead for the first time (she had shared a scene in *Villa Rides* with Mitchum), and Telly Savalas played the villain. Or one of them. It was almost impossible to find anyone to sympathise with in this tale of double-cross, murder, blackmail and more double-cross. Sollima, a Leone disciple with some good spaghetti westerns to his credit, had apparently decided to cut each scene when a cut was least expected, and so give the film as disjointed a feel as possible. If this was his intention, he succeeded. There was the usual excellent score from Morricone, and some memorable scenes, particularly the one in which Ireland and partner fall to their deaths in an external glass elevator, mutely mouthing their despair. The audience must have sympathised with them. Bronson just walked through his part as a stone-faced avenger, communicating nothing save raw purpose and murderous effectiveness.

His next part was not so dissimilar. In *Cold Sweat* he played a Humphrey Bogart-style character, a man with a boat for hire and a shady past.

74

He also has a wife (Liv Ullman) and a stepdaughter, both blissfully unaware of said shady past. The latter, of course, catches up with him, in the form of the two fellow ex-cons (whom he once betrayed for suitably unimpeachable reasons) and the gunhappy maniac they have in tow. He breaks the neck of one pursuer, but the other (James Mason) then kidnaps his wife and stepdaughter. He then kidnaps Mason's mistress (Jill Ireland) and proposes a swap. This goes awry, etc., etc. Bronson looks alternately tough and concerned-for-family, Ullman looks concerned and Mason oozes smarmy malevolence. The gunhappy maniac, played with great relish by Jean Topart, scares all of them.

One American critic put it thus—'abysmally written, harshly overdubbed, and with photographic development that would flunk the film out of a Kiwanis home movie contest, *Cold Sweat* is almost beyond belief'. This was rather harsh; the film's main claim to fame was its almost complete forgetability. And yet Bronson was paid $400,000 for his performance, eight times what he had received for *Villa Rides* a mere three years before.

The bad run continued. *Someone Behind the Door* found him playing an amnesiac who is persuaded by a psychiatrist (Anthony Perkins) into believing that he is the husband of the psychiatrist's unfaithful wife, and that he wants to kill her. There was obviously a dearth of plots around. Perkins twitched nervously as only he can, and Bronson looked suitably confused. It was his fourth undistinguished film in a row.

For the moment it didn't seem to matter. The three films which had produced the breakthrough, and particularly *Once Upon A Time in the West*, were still packing in European audiences. And now Japan was falling under his spell. In a few short months he moved from being virtually unknown to embodying the quintessential 'Western Man', and a billboard three blocks long was adorned with his weathered visage in downtown Tokyo. He even agreed to do a TV commercial for a Japanese corporation, selling a male toiletry, appropriately named 'Mandom'. For four days' work he was paid $100,000, the amount he had received for *The Magnificent Seven* and *The Great Escape* put together. The corporation had no regrets though; within weeks of the commercial hitting the air the product had become the top-seller in its field.

In the long run, however, making bad movies would cost him the newly-won status. He had lost touch with the persona which had proved so successful. None of the four characters he had played since *Passager de la Pluie* had possessed that mythical, larger-than-life dimension. None of the toughness seemed to conceal a more human reality. There was no sense of humour emphasising a detachment from the world, no hint of an inner certainty born in harsh struggle. Bronson had to re-discover such characters and re-assert the persona, if he wasn't to slide from grace as swiftly as he had risen.

Link and Kuroda

THE NEXT FILM, *Red Sun (Soleil Rouge)*, was a curious hybrid, part Leonesque, part traditional western. The opening scene was pure Leone: a station in the middle of nowhere, a train approaching, whistling mournfully. It might be a re-make of *Once Upon A Time in the West*. The train pulls in, only this time round Bronson is waiting for it, complete with new moustache, longer hair and weathered buckskin jacket. He doesn't get aboard straight away, preferring to lean against a building in the shadows, casting a watchful eye along the train. On the verandah of one coach a man of distinctly non-western pedigree appears; he is dresssed in the traditional costume of the Japanese samurai warrior. His and Bronson's eyes meet; they measure each other, so encapsulating the theme of the film. Though different, they are two of a kind. A gentle musical theme plays; it will also be used at the end when one dies in the arms of the other.

The traditional western takes over. The initial explanations are made—the samurai is one of two escorting the new Imperial Ambassador to Washington, Bronson is the leader of a gang intent on robbing the train. This robbery is successful, and in the process the characters of the gang's two dominant personalities, Link (Bronson) and Gauche (Delon), are established. Link is the world-weary humorous type—'my assistants are going to take up a collection, just like they do in church,' he tells the startled passengers—while Gauche is clearly devoid of the humanity which makes such humour possible. Link sees killing as a trick of the trade, but Gauche actually enjoys it.

After cleaning out the train, including the ceremonial sword which the Ambassador is taking as a gift from Emperor to President, Gauche double-crosses Link, thinks he has succeeded in killing him, and makes off with the rest of the gang. Link is left without his hard-robbed money, the Japanese without their sword. The surviving samurai Kuroda (Toshiro Mifune) is charged with the latter's recovery, and Link is persuaded, at sword-point, to help him in the search for Gauche.

All this is rather contrived; if Gauche is the sort of man who'd kill Link without a second thought, then his sparing of the defiant Kuroda makes no sense whatsoever. Still, it gets Bronson and Mifune together, and we're back in less conventional territory. Gunless and horseless they set out after Gauche, and Link is forced to make a re-appraisal of the 'man in the skirt'. He can kill mosquitoes with a swish of his sword, and he proves more than able when it comes to unarmed combat. Link goads him into a 'fistfight'—'my luck's changing,' he remarks somewhat prematurely — and gets thrown on his back with distressing regularity. 'We'll call it a draw,' he says, after landing upside down in the dirt for the umpteenth time. This whole sequence is notable for its humour. But it's not just funny—rarely has the western hero's dependence on his gun been so ruthlessly lampooned.

Link soon gets a new gun, as the two of them take on seven stray members of Gauche's gang at a remote ranch. While casing the joint they watch the rancher refuse to disclose the whereabouts of his daughters. 'A brave man,' says Kuroda, just before the gang shoot the rancher. 'A stupid one,' Link replies. He knows this country, and Kuroda's samurai code of honour is shown to be rather out of place. So is his sword, for no matter how effectively he wields it, spearing nasties like suckling pigs, it can't help him much against a gun at ten paces.

Link is impressed nevertheless, and offers to do a deal. He'll take Kuroda along if the samurai promises not to kill Gauche before the whereabouts of the money has been discovered. Again the samurai code gets in the way—Kuroda is honour-bound to avenge his fellow samurai immediately—and Link decides to part company. This proves easier imagined than done.

The cultural cross-fertilisation continues. Kuroda explains his code, the 'Code of Bushido', and Link replies that 'these days a lot of people have peculiar ideas'. But Kuroda's ideas are anything but peculiar to habitual western-watchers. When he says that 'all has changed... Japan has become a different country... soon a great nation like yours... then samurai life will finish... all must give up swords, become farmers, fishermen, become nothing' he is echoing the words of another ancient race, the western hero, whether white or red. Gun or sword, it makes no difference ('we all die the same way,' he says earlier), what does matter is that the old life, the old *untamed* life is slipping away, leaving the warrior stranded, without identity, just one more face in a sea of worker-ants. Kuroda, like 'Harmonica', must remain true to his code, no matter the cost, because without it he is nothing, no longer a man as he understands manhood.

Link understands this, but is continually distracted by his desire to lay hands on the gold (America in microcosm). The film then moves on through a battle in a whorehouse, and two set-piece encounters with Comanches, to the final showdown. Here Kuroda finally comes up against the sword's inadequacy, and is shot down by Gauche. Link has to choose between honour and gold; he decides for the former, coldly executing the injured Gauche and so abandoning his chance of finding the money. The dying Kuroda, in a neat piece of role reversal, tells Link that he's been stupid. But Link knows better. When Kuroda expresses surprise at Link's willingness to return the sword despite the risk of capture, the American warrior says 'hell, I ain't got nothing else to do'. They are, in the end, indisputably two of a kind.

Red Sun is, in a sense, Mifune's film; his character dominates it in the way that the Bronson's character dominated *Once Upon A Time in the West*. Bronson was here cast in the Robards role, but his performance was so well sustained that the developing partnership between the men, and Link's discovery of his own buried code, his identity, is completely believable. His acting had never been better.

Red Sun has its faults, too many to make it the classic it could have been. The plot left something to be desired, the climactic showdown was not sufficiently imaginative, the Comanche attacks could have been taken from a dozen 'B' westerns. The one haunting theme apart, the music sounds like *The Magnificent Seven* meet *Cleopatra* in *The Big Country*—never did a western more obviously need a Morricone score. Alain Delon's Gauche was too stereotyped, Ursula Andress as his mistress largely superfluous.

But despite such faults, *Red Sun* is a great western. The dialogue is mostly first-rate, the Bronson-Mifune chemistry is just right, and there is a powerful sense of history seeping through the characters and the action. The final scene of the train approaching the station, and the golden sword hanging from the telegraph wires like an eagle perched on a tower-block, would have graced any western, even Leone at his best.

Chato

IN 1970 BRITISH director Michael Winner had made his first western, *Lawman*. In one scene US Marshal Maddox (Burt Lancaster) has his horse shot out from under him by the fleeing Adams (Robert Duvall). The unruffled Maddox unloads his horse, steals two more, and proceeds with the hunt. He has total confidence in his own ability; there is a relentless certainty about Adams' capture.

This scene gave screenplay writer Gerald Wilson the idea for a full-length film, in which one hunted man would become the hunter by virtue of his knowledge of the terrain and the confidence which such knowledge inspired. Winner liked the idea, and sought financial backing for the film, provisionally titled *Chato's Land*. He was going to use an unknown Indian in the lead role, but the studio demanded a star. 'They said they'd finance if I got Charlie to play the part... I didn't mind using Bronson. He has the perfect physique, the perfect body-moves; he moves as if he's really off the land. Not like Jeff Hunter with make-up.'

Bronson was willing, for two main reasons. Particularly now that Jill was pregnant with their first child, he wanted to spend as much time as possible with his family, and Winner had a reputation as a director who got films made quickly. Secondly, he accepted the role because 'I wanted to play an Indian as an Indian should be played. I've not seen an Indian played realistically on the screen yet... I want to give a good, clean-cut and fair identification...'

The film opens conventionally enough. Pardon Chato, an Apache half-breed, is enjoying a quiet drink in a pretty desolate saloon when the local sheriff starts displaying his prejudices. He baits, and eventually tries to kill, Chato. The Indian shoots him down and disappears into the surrounding desert. Back in town a posse is formed, complete with all the requisite characters—the war veteran eager for new glories, the local psychopath-rancher,·the moderate with scruples, the despised Mexican who can read trail-signs, etc. As they set off after Chato these divisions are subsumed in the excitement of the hunt. They will re-appear when things start to go wrong.

When the posse reaches Chato's desert home, his wife is raped and staked out as bait. Chato rescues her, but his friend is burnt alive by the vengeful posse, despite the protestations of some members. The war veteran is slowly losing his authority to the psychopath, and the moderates are thinking, vainly as it turns out, about going home. The hunt continues, but just who is hunting whom becomes unclear, as Chato begins to pick off his pursuers one by one. Internal discord also begins to take a murderous toll. By the end of the film one doomed survivor of the posse wanders helpless in the desert.

This brief plot synopsis does little justice to one of the most powerful westerns of the post-war era. *Chato's Land* works on several levels, as escapist entertainment, as political allegory, and as historical myth. To some extent these three levels were contributed by Winner, Wilson and Bronson respectively, but Winner must take the credit for tying it all together, for seeing that the different contributions were mutually enhancing rather than mutually destructive.

As violent escapism the film is well worked. The suspense is gripping enough, the desert is given second billing to Chato with awesome effect, and Chato himself is seen frequently enough to make him real and rarely enough to give him a quality that is almost superhuman. Despite some reviews to the contrary, the violence is never gratuitous. A film about savagery has to be savage.

Good escapism is necessarily timeless (that is to say, removed from historical time), but *Chato's Land* manages to be timeful as well. This was 1971, year six of the American assault on Vietnam. Screenplay-writer Wilson, according to Winner in an interview given to film biographer Bill Harding, 'saw *Chato's Land* as a parallel with Vietnam or any other powerful country trying to impose its way of life on another. It's about a country that gets into a situation of guerrilla warfare, fighting a local culture which it goes against, convinced its size will make it win, and finds that in fact the local culture is stronger, and it's destroying itself... both militarily and emotionally. It was intended as a deliberate parallel with Vietnam. There's an interesting point in how many people spotted that. The French critics spotted it almost to a man; the Germans and Italians spotted it to a man. Four or five Americans spotted it.'

It's hard to imagine how most American critics missed it; the parallel was as obvious as it was deliberate. Into a foreign country march the whites, both hawks and doves, carrying each his baggage of prejudices, all full of a passionate belief in their own power and righteousness. And one by one, at each other's and the enemy's hand, they fall. There was nothing subtle about the handling of this theme, no deep characterisation, no profound analysis. There was only relevance. It was something that needed to be said in a popular context.

Bronson himself had not been a noted opponent of the war; with his traditionalistic and nationalistic views he was probably quietly in favour. What he brought to *Chato's Land* was a recreation, in different guise, of the persona developed in *Once Upon A Time in the West* and *Red Sun*, the individual whose rigid self-control enables him to escape the control of others.

In *Chato's Land* this self-control both implies and depends upon his ability to 'control' the land, to survive in the desert. The posse lacks this ability, and so loses its self-control. Unlike Kuroda and Link in *Red Sun*, Chato is fighting on ground where the old values still hold undisputed sway, where there's still no skill like an old skill. In the wilderness only an individual untrammelled by civilisation can win. Chato is only vulnerable at his one, civilised, point—his place of settlement. There the posse can bring its power to bear, just as the US forces in Vietnam could control the villages. But in the desert or jungle the edge is with the other side, and a refusal to realise as much is liable to be fatal.

Bronson might merely have wanted to play an Indian 'as an Indian should be played', but he brought more to the part than that. A star is almost always the persona he or she has built up through the accumulation of related roles, and Bronson's Chato fused earlier characters into one defiant figure. Nobility is the word that springs to mind, an old-fashioned concept for an ancient race. Bronson had only fifteen lines of dialogue in the film, thirteen of them in Apache dialect, but despite, or because of, this lack of 'civilised' articulacy, the legendary nature of his persona becomes all the clearer. Alternately magical and cruel beyond the imagination of the 'civilised' posse, his victory is one for the past over the future, for the sensitivity and savagery of humanity in its long-lost natural state over a civilisation which measures its cruelties and represses all sensitivity.

No other actor could have played Pardon Chato with such force, could have given the film such a cumulative resonance. If *Once Upon A Time in the West* and *Red Sun* were shared triumphs, *Chato's Land* was his and his alone. He had made it work.

PART FOUR

COUNTENANCE OF
STONE

'The Sexiest Man in the World'

LATE IN 1971 Bronson started work on *The Mechanic (Killer of Killers)*, his second film with Michael Winner, and his first Hollywood movie for almost five years. Though still hardly a major star in the United States, his popularity beyond the land of his birth was now such that the American industry could no longer afford to ignore him.

Dramatic proof of this popularity was provided by a Reuter's poll of sixty countries early in 1972, which showed Bronson and Sean Connery sharing the position of the world's most loved film star. Since Connery's ranking reflected the success of the Bond films rather than his own undoubted acting ability, Bronson had every reason to consider himself the no. 1. Famous columnist Rex Reed noted, to the amazement of many Americans, that 'Charles Bronson is the only star whose name alone brings a guaranteed budget of a million dollars minimum on an unfinished screenplay. . .'

As 1972 progressed, poll after poll confirmed the Reuter result. In France the 'Holy Monster' had outstripped Belmondo, in Italy the 'Ugly One' had vanquished Mastroianni. In Spain matador El Cordobes was knocked off the primo sex symbol perch. Europe had been conquered, and like a world war the ripples were spreading. In Japan, Bronson shared top spot with *Red Sun* co-star Toshiro Mifune, in South America he was simply announced to be the world's sexiest man.

What did Bronson think of all this? For one thing, he had few doubts as to the reason for his sudden lurch to global fame. Leaving America had been the decisive step. If he had stayed, 'I would probably have been stuck in featured roles. . . Hollywood has always been limited in the casting of stars. The money for films is borrowed on the stars' names, and traditionally the stars have been the half-baked publicity names. In Europe there is no such problem. Most of the countries have government subsidies, so the producers don't have to borrow on their stars' names. They hire the best actors for the roles. It's sad about Hollywood. There are a few hundred actors around this town who are capable of leading roles. What are they doing? Selling encyclopaedias, I guess.'

The American industry, run by 'petty tyrants . . . the kind who only work in a fraught atmosphere, whipping up everyone against everyone else', was, according to Bronson, too inward-looking, too 'nationalistic'. Once the purveyor of entertainment to the whole developed world, it was now busy investigating the American navel, making films which were exclusively aimed at American audiences. In Europe, on the other hand, films were being made for the world market, with the result that more money was available, particularly for the stars. 'In Europe I get my full salary where I want it—upfront. . . In America no matter how big a star you are, you're asked to take a cut in salary of a third to a half and accept a percentage. . .'

The 'petty tyrants' of Hollywood did not, in Bronson's view, treat actors with the respect they deserved. Admittedly the Europeans were a little over-respectful in their attitude towards directors, but this was a far more congenial habit than the American one of treating only the money-men with respect. Bronson was enjoying the big star treatment accorded him in the Far East and Europe, and he contrasted it somewhat bitterly with 'the calloused jaded attitude towards actors' in the United States. In Hollywood, 'they've seen them come and go for years and they just don't give a damn about them. . . People behind the scenes, in production offices, finance and legal departments, couldn't care less about actors. Their attitude is wrong. Everyone's bread and butter ultimately depends upon whether or not the actor delivers. Despite the many creative off-camera talents which go into making a film, what the audience sees on that screen is the actor. What the performer brings to the part, how he interprets the dialogue, what special talents he employs to make the production come alive and be meaningful, that's what counts. If that weren't true, the whole industry would consist of animated cartoons.'

Some would say that the big US movie companies, increasingly geared to TV, were turning out just that, with Starsky and Hutch as a latter-day version of Tom and Jerry. 'If money doesn't talk, it swears' as Dylan once observed. But to someone like Bronson this secularising of Hollywood was profoundly unwelcome. He had grown up in an age when stars were worshipped, and it seems likely that deep-down he still believed they should be.

This traditional view was balanced by another, the coal miner's contempt for acting as an unmanly profession, full of 'envy and jealousy and vanity'. Bronson was an actor, he said, because 'acting is the easiest thing I've ever done'. But he felt detached from the whole business. 'To me the whole scene is something I'm passing through... That whole Hollywood bullshit is just amusing to me. I look at it and I laugh. Some actors think it's a big deal to be a star but it's not such a big deal. Basically it's just another way of earning a living, a very pleasant way but nothing more. I don't get fulfilment from being an actor or a star. I get fulfilment from my family.'

Another traditional view. Bronson was, to put it simply, old-fashioned. And the 1970s, unlike the 1960s, had a distinctly ambivalent attitude towards the 'old-fashioned'. Indeed, in large part, Bronson's rising popularity was based on his personalisation of old-style values, on the harking back towards a simplicity which seemed forever lost. Audiences liked heroes who seemed to be in control of their environments, of their destinies, who were not hemmed in by red or blue tape.

Of course, those same audiences didn't like it quite so much when the other face of this mythical world presented itself. Those into conservation didn't like to think of themselves as into conservatism. Someone like Robert Redford, whose cinematic appeal was also largely based on the personification of old-style values, could get away with the balancing trick because he espoused causes that were both traditionalistic and avowedly revolutionary, like ecology. He might live traditionally, enjoy nuclear family life, but he never said anything which the women's movement could take objection to.

Bronson, far less articulate and far more conservatively minded, was not so circumspect. 'If any of the things these Women's Libbers want were to come about,' he said in 1972, 'I would leave America immediately. Women are not equal—never could be.' On wider political matters he usually preferred to remain silent, surfacing every once in a while to hit out at fellow film stars who were using their cinematic eminence to espouse political beliefs. It was more than coincidence, though, that the targets of Bronson's attacks were invariably the 'stars' of the left, like Fonda or Sutherland or Redgrave, and not the luminae of Hollywood's Republican mafia. One attack on the Redford-produced *All The President's Men*—it was 'one-sided philosophy' Bronson said—defied all credibility or sense.

One particular bugbear was nudity in films. 'As far as I'm concerned,' he said in 1972, 'stripping naked is not entertainment. It's for voyeurs, and I'm damn sure I'm not going to feed their imaginations and let them get their kicks from seeing me totally nude.' He now had the clout to enforce such views, and for *The Valachi Papers* two scenes were to be re-written at his insistence. 'I have six kids to think about, and I'm damned if I will show all I've got on the screen and risk them seeing it when they get older. And I don't want other kids talking about it. An actor of my stature doesn't have to worry about doing dirty stuff in films.'

Fair enough, but to go on and suggest that 'other actors do that stuff because if they want work, then they have little choice' showed an alarming narrowness of mind. Doubtless some actors and actresses are forced into making such bargains, but Bronson seemed totally unaware that others, less hidebound by his Victorian-style prejudices, were quite willing to appear nude and to portray sex on the screen, and that there did exist, deep in the bowels of the industry, people who believed that films should try to reflect a reality which included nudity and sex.

Bronson was not only detached from the film world, but also from the world he made films in and for. He lived in two 'places', in the bosom of his family and in the past, in the social milieu of Ehrenfeld. His only idea for a movie which he *really* wanted to make was one set in a mining town in the 1930s, an idea which he and Jill

96

worked at intermittently for years. Both these 'places' were real enough, but neither offered him many clues when it came to understanding the reasons for his sudden success. He knew he had not become an overnight superstar because of his brilliance as an actor; talent in that direction, he knew as well as anyone else, had little to do with commercial success. He didn't associate his new popularity with the violence of many of his films; to him they weren't violent films at all, they were 'action films'. Perhaps, he pondered out loud in later years, young people saw him as a 'father figure. They know about my marriage to Jill, my happy home life and my love of children. Perhaps I fill a void. Many parents have abdicated many of their responsibilities towards raising children—maybe the kids make an idol of someone they feel could give them guidance.'

This was the statement of a sensitive, caring man who hadn't got a clue about the world of the 1970s. Basically he didn't know why the years of trying had suddenly paid off, and most likely, most of the time, he didn't much care. Maybe the gods had simply smiled on him for reasons of their own.

This lack of understanding was unfortunate, for it made him more vulnerable to other people's explanations of his success. *Newsweek* ran a major feature on him, and described his films thus—'the scripts are tommy-guns of cliché in which blood flows like red-eye, and the starlets wear bodices that pop open with the regularity of an exhibitionist's raincoat. But what the audience really digs is Bronson's tough-yet-tender act, which mixes parody and fantasy.'

This 'analysis' was essentially inaccurate. In fact it describes *Newsweek* better than Bronson's work up to 1972. His films had certainly not been pacific, but neither had they been noted for excessive violence, *Once Upon A Time in the West*, for example, was less violent than the 'Dollar Trilogy', and considerably less dependent for its impact on the use of violence. *Red Sun* was not much more violent than *The Magnificent Seven*, an American apple-pie movie if ever there was one, and made ten years earlier. Only *Chato's Land* had really wallowed in blood, and that was a film which could not have been made in any other way.

As for the popping bodices—one of the most notable things about Bronson's starring vehicles was the lack of bodices to pop. His own feelings on this score have been noted, and the more control he secured over his films the less acreage of naked flesh there was. By 1975 it would be down to more or less zero.

The 'tough-yet-tender' bit was closer to the mark, but the point about Bronson was the quality of his tenderness. It was not simply the heart of gold hiding behind the iron exterior, it was the almost animalistic innocence which balanced a savage exterior. This was the dialectic which made Bronson special—he was a Clint Eastwood who looked and sounded convincing talking to children. Take away that dialectic—or completely fail to understand it as *Newsweek*'s critic had done—and all that was left was an in-articulate Eastwood, without the latter's knack for picking good movies or roles.

Filming by numbers

NEWSWEEK'S ANALYSIS, THOUGH wrong in 1972, was to prove almost a self-fulfilling prophecy. What America wanted America got, and America now wanted Bronson back, suitably re-worked for the American market. All the subtlety which had made *Once Upon A Time in the West* a once-in-a-decade movie in Europe and a huge flop in the States—all that had to go. The warmth and humour which had lifted *Red Sun* above the ordinary, the political pertinacity of *Chato's Land*—all that had to go. When Eastwood had returned in triumph to Hollywood, a foreign-made star, Hollywood had created *Hang'em High*, his worst western by far, a plate of spaghetti cooked by people who thought a carbohydrate was just a carbohydrate. The imagination, the humour, the mystery had all disappeared. Only the violence remained. Bronson could expect the same treatment. Robert Mitchum had once remarked that Bronson 'held a pistol well', and the American industry seems to have concluded that that was all he could do. After all, he couldn't have won over

100

all those foreigners with subtlety, now could he?

Michael Winner gave a clue to the transformation of Bronson's persona when describing the opening sequence of *The Mechanic*. 'Nobody spoke for nearly fifteen minutes and we ran the credit titles over some of it. I thought we'd better run something else with it, but it wasn't necessary because of Bronson's wonderful presence.' In the same interview with Bill Harding, Winner noted that 'these action players are underrated. People say all they do is stand there. It's very difficult to stand there and retain the audience's interest.'

This may be so, but 'presence' is more than physical appearance; it grows with a star's career, until each role plays a part in re-defining the others. The Bronson we see in the opening sequence of *The Mechanic* is O'Reilly and Danny and Link and 'Harmonica' and Dobbs—the 'presence' is the presence of them all. The problem, of course, is to keep supplying new inputs, to keep fertilising the persona, to keep it growing. For if this is not done the persona slowly turns into a stereotype, bound by a particular time, and increasingly irrelevant with each new film the star makes.

The Mechanic tells the story of a wise old hitman who takes as an apprentice the son of one of his former victims. The youngster (Jan Michael Vincent) learns enough to kill off the old scorpion, but not enough to escape the posthumous sting. There is a great deal of early-1970s philosophy — 'Murder is only killing without a licence; everybody kills — governments, the

101

military, the police.' Emotion is noticeably absent; even the killings are done by remote control.

It was a straightforward commercial film, with none of the resonance of a *Chato's Land*, violent, tolerably exciting, vaguely distasteful in the relish with which it dissected the assassin's craft. For Bronson it was just a walk-on. For the moment a 'wonderful presence' was enough.

Way back in 1965 he had given an interview to *Cinema* magazine, in which he had talked at length about the difference between acting and starring in movies, between 'character actors and straight actors, meaning a dramatic actor as opposed to an actor who did light things, straight things, without drama'. A character actor, for example, could not play 007. In James Bond movies, Bronson said, or 'in any film that is designed for mass appeal . . . the star, to me, is not an actor. He doesn't do a scene. An actor in that kind of role just wanders through the action. He doesn't impose himself on the action, and that is ideal for the part. Because people imagine that there is more going on in his mind than there actually is, more than he portrays, than he actually acts.' Good actors who became leading men, stars, 'they begin to act like a straight man. They think that's what a leading man is. They begin to go as straight as possible. They make a big hit in a character role, then they are given an opportunity because an audience has liked them. Given an opportunity for something more straight, and a leading credit, and all of a sudden they try to act like they are straight men. It destroys them.'

Bronson should have re-read this interview, because in 1972-3 he was in grave danger of ignoring his own sound advice. *The Mechanic* was not a mistake he could afford to repeat too often.

The next film was *The Valachi Papers*, which dramatised Joe Valachi's testimony to the US Senate concerning half a century of Mafia intrigue. It's easy to see why Bronson was attracted to the part: he would be required to age about forty years, something of a challenge to any character actor. Valachi himself was an interesting figure to someone, like Bronson, who'd grown up on the underside of the American dream. He was, Bronson thought, 'a simple man . . . very human . . . very warm. He grew up in the Mafia, and he joined just to make a living. I'm not idolising him. I just want to show his simplicity and the sad, sad life he was leading. Joe Valachi had no choice but to be a killer. He had nothing to lose.'

It's also easy to see why producer Dino de Laurentiis was interested in making the movie. *The Godfather* had made the Mafia big news at the box-office, and *The Valachi Papers* was also to prove a huge financial success. In most other respects, however, the gulf between the two movies was wide enough to sink the Poseidon in. Terence Young was no Francis Ford Coppola, the screenplay was indifferent, and Bronson, for all his presence, was no Marlon Brando. Not that he had much chance to be. In *The Godfather* the violence had oozed out through characters and plot, in *The Valachi Papers* it was the other way round.

Still, it was Bronson's first major American success, and for that reason alone must have been immensely satisfying. In the meantime he had signed a three-picture contract with de Laurentiis, and begun filming the first of these, *The Valdez Horses*, in Spain. The director was John Sturges once more, and as in *The Magnificent Seven* and *The Great Escape* Bronson played a more than usually sympathetic character. Chino Valdez loves horses, kids and Red Indians, and you can't get much more sympathetic than that. In the end he even restrains himself from seeing off the villainous neighbour, rather than put his favourite horse at risk. An interesting lightweight movie, *The Valdez Horses* arrested Bronson's slide without reversing it.

However, that could not be said of his next two offerings. *The Stone Killer*, his third film with Michael Winner, had precious little to recommend it. A *Dirty Harry*-style movie without its precursor's style or moral ambivalence, *The Stone Killer* featured another vigilante-type policeman wandering homicidally through that world of ethnic junkies, homosexual trombonists, Mafia conspiracies and epic car chases which the film industry likes to think passes for an exciting collage of contemporary America. Bronson played the policeman, one Detective Torrey, whose stone-faced determination to prevent a Mafia reprisal massacre—why? one wonders—leads him into trouble with both underworld perverts/ killers and his po-faced and dangerously liberal/ corrupt superiors. Women are conspicuous by their absence in this world. Torrey seems to have no motivation save the script, which apparently consists of an obituary column complete with camera angles.

If Detective Torrey was simply *The Mechanic* shifted across the invisible border of legality, *Mr Majestyk* was a Chino Valdez who grew melons rather than horses. He refuses to take the bad guy's exploited migrant workers, preferring free, slightly less exploited, smiling migrant workers to pick his ripening melons. The bad guy frames him on an assault charge, but en route for jail he finds himself sharing the police bus with another bad guy, a Mafia assassin. The latter is about to be rescued, but when the ambush takes place Majestyk manages to kidnap the assassin, etc., etc. Eventually the two bad guys join forces, but Majestyk, remembering Chato's trick, lures them into country he knows and disposes of them. He then returns to his melons and the smiling workeress (Linda Crystal).

It's entertaining enough, good for two hours in front of the TV, though hardly worth the price of a cinema ticket. There's nothing *special* about it; it's as if Bronson's persona has been shrunk to fit the TV screen and the TV mentality. As David McGillivray put it: 'Chino Valdez alias Mr Majestyk alias The Mechanic alias Pardon Chato is a morose loner of uncertain origins, who loves simple things but is dangerous when riled. Any other details seem to fall into place around this obdurate image.'

Bronson's persona had become stereotyped. To make room for the action, characterisation had been sacrificed. The film-makers thought they could get away with this because in Bronson they had a ready-made character, one who needed only to narrow his eyes or fondle an animal to evoke memories of all that character's previous incarnations. But this simple reliance on superficial character-traits, carried over from film to film, grew more and more boring. For a while audiences would flock to see the new Bronson movie because they knew exactly what to expect, but after a while longer they would stay away for precisely the same reason. Obviously the essential traits of the character could no longer be changed without risking everything, but something had to be done in the way of refurbishment. The next role needed to have more depth, and had to relate more directly to the reality of America in the mid-1970s. Bronson had to re-attach his persona to history.

Social work in New York

BRONSON'S GUARDIAN ANGEL, who had been none too active in the 1960s, was now working overtime. When the star first glanced through the script of *Death Wish* he was probably struck by the ease with which it fitted into the now-established formula. The Paul Kersey character was quickly turned into a morose loner by circumstance, and once riled proved acceptably dangerous. There was no obvious reason why the film should become a sensation.

The pre-credit sequence simultaneously established a world and pointed to its vulnerability. Paul Kersey (Bronson) and his wife (Hope Lange) are a middle-aged couple on holiday in sunny Hawaii, taking snapshots on the beach, clearly still very much in love with each other. They feel like consummating the emotion there and then, but inhibitions dictate a retreat to the hotel room. Kersey jokingly remembers a time when they weren't quite so civilised. Soon it won't be a joking matter.

They return to New York, all traffic, dirt and

mugging statistics. Kersey's wife and married daughter do some shopping, and three manic youths read the address on the delivery package. They bluff their way into the Kersey apartment, rape the daughter and carelessly kill the mother. The police hold out no hope of capturing the youths responsible; it's just one more crime, one more reason for the wringing of hands.

Kersey's firm—he is an architect with 'liberal' opinions—sends him to do a job in Arizona, partly as a way of getting his mind off the tragedy. The developer he works with there, Ames (Stuart Margolin), takes him to a Wild West show, a simulated encounter between the brave US Marshal ('honest men with dreams who could fight to protect their womenfolk' says the accompanying commentary) and several no-good cowboys, looking for 'a short cut to easy money'. The parallel could hardly be more explicitly drawn.

Next Ames takes Kersey to the local gun club, only to find that his new friend was a conscientious objector in the Korean War (Kersey really *is* a liberal). Ames, undeterred, tells him that 'out here I hardly know a man who doesn't own a gun. And I tell you something—unlike your city, we can walk our streets and through our parks at night. Muggers operating out here, they'd just plain get their asses blown off.'

And, surprise surprise, the conscientious objector can shoot. His father had been a crackshot, his mother a Quaker, and once the former had been killed in a hunting accident son Paul had given up guns for good. Until now, that is. Returning to New York, Kersey is met by son-in-law Jack at the airport. His daughter hasn't got over the shock—'she's almost a goddam veget-able' Jack tells him. The police have got nowhere, will get nowhere. Wife and daughter are 'just statistics on a police blotter', Jack says, 'and there's nothing we can do to stop it, nothing but cut and run'. Back at his apartment Kersey discovers that Ames' goodbye present is a gun.

He goes for a walk in the neighbourhood park, a mugger attempts to hold him up, and Kersey shoots him down. It's not easy for the conscien-tious objector to accept; back in the apartment his hand shakes, he croaks 'Jesus, Jesus Christ', and vomits. Killing doesn't come naturally to the civilised.

It's easier the second time. He stumbles across a mugging-in-progress and shoots all three muggers dead. Soon after this the film's key con-versation takes place between him and the unsuspecting Jack:

KERSEY: Nothing to do but cut and run, uh? What about the old American custom of self-defence? If the police don't defend us maybe we ought to do it ourselves.
JACK: We're not pioneers anymore, dad.
KERSEY: What are we, Jack? I mean, if we're not pioneers, what have we become. What do you call people, who when they're faced with a condition of fear, do nothing about it. They just run and hide.
JACK: Civilised?
KERSEY: (after long pause) No. . .

From this point on Kersey goes out looking for muggers, using himself as the bait and then

109

shooting them down. The police want him to stop (freelance law enforcement is not on), but they don't want to catch him, because the mugging rate in the city has fallen in response to his one-man campaign.

Kersey himself is busy mutating into an untamed individual. He paints his apartment in bright colours, plays music at deafening volume, and generally gives the air of someone who's happy with his work. All the guilt is gone. More and more he comes to resemble a western hero, calling on one mugger to 'fill your hand . . . draw'. When the police inspector orders him to leave New York he ironically murmurs 'By sundown?'

Death Wish is not a subtle movie. Indeed, it would be hard to find a film for which the word 'blatant' seems so apt. Everything is neatly arranged, each point is hammered home with words, pictures and music. The muggers—at least, the initial group who kill Kersey's wife—are not simple, violent souls, let alone the maligned children of inner city deprivation. They are cackling maniacs, in love with spray-cans, more like animals than humans. Kersey himself is constructed to fit the story—he must be able to shoot, he must be sensitive enough to grab the audience's sympathy. So the ridiculous history of the dead-eye conscientious objector is created.

But despite all this, despite the way in which Winner and script seek so blatantly to manipulate the emotions of the audience, *Death Wish* manages to feel realistic. There are enough solid facts, enough emotional truth on display to make the film work. The audience knows Kersey's initial impotence in the face of such tragedy, it knows that there are maniacs wandering the streets, and that the police are helpless. After all, it doesn't much matter if inner city decay and deprivation create crime when the consequences are standing right in front of you with a knife. Most important of all, the audience knows that someone acting, successfully, the way Kersey does as a one-man vigilante army, *would* bring down the mugging statistics, *would* make old ladies feel a little safer on the streets. It is this which gives *Death Wish* its claim to authenticity, its cutting edge.

Film-makers had brought frontier values to bear in New York before, most notably in the Siegel-Eastwood movie *Coogan's Bluff*. But in this earlier film the character of Coogan, an Arizona lawman come to the Big Apple to collect a prisoner, is not allowed to develop. He is simply the West, the frontier, personified. Kersey, by contrast, discovers the frontier within himself, albeit with a little prodding from Ames. He has to develop for the picture to work.

Most of the credit for the film's credibility thus belonged to Bronson. His acting skills had never been seen to greater effect. He was convincing as the tender husband, the bereaved and confused husband and father, the agonised conscientious objector turned killer and, needless to say, the man of action. And audiences loved the character; here was someone doing what they'd

111

like to do—fight back. In New York cinemas each slaying of a mugger was greeted by cheering in the stalls.

The critics either loved or, mostly, hated it. 'A streetside fascist potboiler' one critic called it, admitting apologetically that it was all done 'with such slambang effectiveness that it has the power to shrink, at least momentarily, intellectual distance.' An interesting comment. What intellectual distance was being shrunk? Brian Garfield, writer of the novel on which the film was based, thought the essential difference 'between the book and the movie is that the book suggests that this kind of thing could happen and that it's a dangerous possibility. The movie suggests not only that it could happen, but that it *ought* to happen.'

This seems like a writer's sleight of hand. The message of *Death Wish* seems crystal-clear—if you want to survive in the new wilderness then you can't afford a civilised code of behaviour. Obviously there are two, and only two, answers to such a situation—you either throw off moral restraints or you civilise the wilderness. In the face of modern society's refusal to do anything about the conditions which breed such crime—poverty, racial prejudice, commercialisation of anything that moves, TV 'entertainment', gun availability, and all the other things which add up to the general and lethal alienation of large sections of the so-called community —then someone like Kersey can only, as the film says, either 'cut and run' or fight back as an individual. It's a real problem. The directness with which it was presented was what made *Death Wish* one of the most important movies of the decade.

Bronson, as usual, was loth to talk philosophy. When questioned about the 'meaning' of the film, he simply announced that 'it had never come up'. He did admit that agent Kohner had disagreed with him over accepting the role. 'Paul felt very strongly that it was a dangerous picture—that it might make people think it's right to take the law into their own hands. I told Paul I thought the message was the same theme that runs through a lot of my pictures: that violence is senseless because it only begets more violence.' His only initial worry was that the part was written as 'a meek little New York accountant. I thought it was a much better picture for Dustin Hoffman. It was the director, Michael Winner, who talked me into doing the movie. He said he could change the part to a more active and virile architect and we'd all make a potful of money.'

They did indeed. Bronson had finally conquered America.

PART FIVE

THE
FAMILIAR STRANGER

A rut lined with dollars

ALL THE HULLABALOO surrounding *Death Wish* left
Bronson unmoved. He had no desire to make
'fascist' movies or 'social comment' movies of any
kind; in his view the sort of movies he made had
little or nothing to do with the world beyond the
cinema. 'What I'm doing isn't art,' he said, 'it's
entertainment.' And that was all. 'I'm not in
movies for social reform. I'm in films for the
money.'

Bob Dylan used to say such things in the mid-
1960s. At a time when his music, and particularly
his lyrics, seemed to be opening mental and emotional doors for a generation, he would insist that
he was 'just a folk-singer', that all he wanted from
the world was enough money to 'buy a new pair
of boots'. Of course no one believed him—there
was too much intelligence, too much calculation
at work in his music, and the denial of a message
was clearly a part of the message.

Bronson, even at his peak, was not a compar-
able figure, but he had made films that raised
enough questions in enough interesting ways for

them to qualify as 'art', or at least as more than mere entertainment. But when the actor denied any intention of providing more than entertainment, he meant it. He really believed his films were just that, a pleasant diversion for the cinema-going public. And despite the evidence, which suggested that the more thoughtful his films were, the more popular they were, he continued to ascribe his success to the more predictable elements they contained, the 'father figure' image, the all-out 'action', the excellence of his 'pistol-holding'. *Death Wish*, to him, was simply more of the same. It didn't seem to occur to him that its astonishing success was dependent on two new factors. First, he had played out of his usual character, had played an ordinary human being *turning into* his usual character, so connecting the ordinary world inhabited by his audience to the extraordinary world inhabited by his movie persona. Second, this transformation of an individual had been catalysed by a real social situation which concerned ordinary people. The character had changed for them.

These things can't have occurred to him, because if they had he would not have gone on to make the movies that he did. Doubtless he was not alone in making this 'mistake'; the people who offered him million dollar fees for churning out routine action yarns were as short-sighted as he was. Even Michael Winner could say that Bronson was 'popular because he has chosen in his career to make films on a commercial basis, whereas other stars like Steve McQueen and Paul

Newman have tried to add art to their films'. The whole Hollywood establishment liked to believe that art was wonderful and that non-art was what made money. The public reaction proved it—crap was popular. It never occurred to them that the public might go for something which bridged the gap, because the public was hardly ever given the choice. When the artier popular movies, like *Apocalypse Now, The Deer Hunter* or *Ordinary People*, proved commercially successful, they were just put down as exceptions to the rule.

But, it must be said, Bronson was now big enough to dispense with such logic if he felt the urge. For the next few years anything he made would pull in the crowds on the one hand and the necessary financing on the other. Either way he would capitalise on his new status in the sense of making 'potfuls of money', but only by taking the more difficult route, by choosing films that stretched both his talents and the normally-accepted parameters of Hollywood commerciality, could he raise himself into a figure of real cinematic importance. It was here that he failed. The next three films, though good, solid entertainment, were basically unadventurous. He had settled for the easy option.

The first of these, *Breakout*, was an action yarn set astride the US-Mexican border, with Bronson cast as Nick Colton, a hirer and flier of planes and helicopters enlisted by Ann Wagner (Jill Ireland) to break husband Jay (Robert Duvall) out of a Mexican jail. John Huston played the charmingly villainous father, and the CIA, not unusually for the mid-1970s, took the role of eminence grise.

The character of Nick Colton was superficially similar to that of Link in *Red Sun*—amiable, garrulous (for a Bronson part), and far from infallible—but he had no Kuroda to challenge his sense of self or purpose. At the end of *Breakout* there is no sign that he has been changed by his adventure. A suspicion exists that he was trying for a Humphrey Bogart-style persona—the plot parallels with *To Have and Have Not* are striking—but if so he lacked the range. Bronson can display an underlying tenderness, but not an underlying vulnerability. You never get the feeling that he's living on the edge of his own personality, that self-containment is being forced upon him. He's too solid, and he enjoys it too much.

Hard Times (The Streetfighter) found him back on more familiar territory. Prizefighter Chaney wasn't amiable, garrulous or fallible. He was tough (in the ring) and tender (with hooker Lucy); the film might have been sub-titled 'Chato meets the Great Depression'. Like *Breakout* it was an entertaining film, ideal for an evening's night out or two hours, TV with the beer cans piling up. There was plenty of violence, some well-acted stereotypes, and a nice eye for period detail. And for some strange reason the critics liked it. 'Surprise: a good Charles Bronson movie', said *Time*. 'The best thing he's ever done', said the *New York Daily News*. Praise was showered on first-time director Walter Hill (later famous for *The Warriors*, etc.) and, with rather more reason, on Bronson for agreeing to work with him. As the producer observed: 'There aren't many super-stars who will work with a first-time director.'

If this made *Hard Times* a rather risky venture by Bronson standards, the next effort was about as riskless as movies get. *Breakheart Pass* was written by Alistair MacLean—those last four words were guaranteed to bring in the money and the audiences. Everyone knew what to expect: a series of irrational happenings (usually deaths), two twists of the plot (close together so as to maximise the confusion), and the triumphant emergence of the real hero, who wins through, saves humanity (or a portion thereof) and gets the woman (if there's one to be got). *Breakheart Pass* disappointed no one, and for the benefit of those who missed it, but who have seen other MacLean movies, it can be confided that the action takes place on a train in the American West. Armed with this information, it should be possible to reconstruct the whole film mentally.

bronson walked through it as the mysterious outlaw/marshal who knows what is happening when the audience doesn't. And why not? The film, like his previous two, brought the dollars rolling in. And not only for him. Wife Jill had been in all three movies—none-too-impressive in *Breakout*, excellent in *Hard Times*, competent in *Breakheart Pass*—and her $75,000 fees provided icing for Charlie's million dollar cakes. For those three-and-a-quarter million dollars the couple had worked a total of twenty-one weeks. It was a long long way from Ehrenfeld.

Wasting assets

IN RETROSPECT THE comedy western *From Noon Til Three* looks like a conscious attempt to escape the deepening rut, but since that rut was still proving lucrative, it seems more likely that the Bronsons simply felt like a change. He plays Dorsey, leader of a gang of bank-robbers, she the obliging widow who cares for his wants when a lame horse prevents him taking part in the planned robbery. His comrades-in-crime get caught, and the widow, catching the spirit of the thing, sends him off to effect a gallant rescue. But by this time he has lost the spirit of the thing, and rides off in the opposite direction. He swaps clothes with an intinerant dentist, who is then shot by the posse hunting Dorsey. Meantime, Dorsey has been arrested and jailed for the dentist's crimes. When he emerges from incarceration a few years later he finds himself the central character in a legend spun by the widow. She shoots herself rather than betray her own legend, and he's committed to an asylum for claiming to be who he is.

It was a good script on paper, and since writer

Frank D. Gilroy also directed, it wasn't easy to pinpoint the reasons for the film's failure. For failure it was, both with the critics and at the box-office. Some of the former exculpated Bronson, even praised him for his comic touch, but few thought much of Jill Ireland's performance or Gilroy's directorial skills. *From Noon Til Three* can hardly have encouraged Bronson to stray too far from his rut.

The next five movies, made in the period 1975-7, were all firmly grounded in familiar territory. *St Ives* featured Bronson as a novelist drawn through lack of funds into a web of criminal intrigue, complete with bodies in spin-driers, bodies plummeting from hotel windows, bodies shot full of holes and bodies belonging to Jacqueline Bisset. Bronson wanders through this world of bodies, and an incredibly convoluted plot, in usual taciturn style. Any hint of character had obviously been carefully eliminated in the editing room.

Raid on Entebbe was one of three films made about the hijacking to Uganda of an Air France plane and the subsequent Israeli rescue operation in the summer of 1976. Bronson played Brigadier-General Dan Shomron, the commander of the operation, a part which required no more than the normal stiff-lipped effectiveness. That said, *Raid on Entebbe* was far and away the best of the three movies, truer to the facts than the Israeli film and not drowned in sentiment like the other Hollywood product, *Victory at Entebbe*.

After playing this cameo role Bronson must

123

have wanted something larger-than-life. He found it. *The White Buffalo* is a film which every aspiring writer, director, cameraman or actor should study at length. It is a veritable manual of cinematic disasters. A ludicrous story, bad direction, bad acting by a group of normally excellent actors, dialogue which must have burnt the tongue and special effects which are special to the point of rank incompetence.

The plot—believe it if you can—concerns the search for a huge albino buffalo in Wyoming *circa* 1974. Wild Bill Hickok (Bronson) now lives back East, but finds himself troubled by a recurring nightmare in which the said buffalo charges straight at him (why?—you never find out why). Meanwhile, out on the prairie, Crazy Horse (Will Sampson, fresh from great performances in *The Outlaw Josey Wales* and *One Flew Over The Cuckoo's Nest*) finds that his baby daughter has been killed by the beast. His father re-names him Worm, and tells him that he won't get his real name back until he brings home the albino pelt. Hickok has by this time reached the area, got into trouble with Whistling Jack Killeen (Clint Walker), rediscovered old friend Charlie Zane (Jack Warden) and revisited old flame Poker Jenny (Kim Novak). After many scrapes—the script seems almost visible at times—Hickok and Crazy Horse get down to the serious business of saving each other's lives and disposing of the title beast, which looks like a shaggy white carpet mounted on wheels.

Hickok survives, but Bronson comes close to

going down with his own Moby Dick. The film's one saving feature is the murkiness of the photography, which makes it hard to see. As one critic observed: 'It is an alltime low for the indestructible Bronson, who cannot even rely on his dourfaced macho to pull him through. . .'

Following this with something worse was going to be difficult, and not surprisingly the next film represented a considerable improvement. For once Bronson chose to work with an actress, Lee Remick, and a director, Don Siegel, who were more than merely competent. This might not seem such a great deal, but one of the most pertinent factors influencing Bronson's output in the 1970s had been the calibre of his leading ladies and directors. In the sixteen films made since *Cold Sweat*, in itself Liv Ullman's direst hour, he had lacked a leading lady on seven occasions, employed wife Jill on seven others, and used Jacqueline Bisset and Linda Crystal once each. And while none of these three ladies could be called a bad actress, it is certainly true that none of them offered any competition on the screen to Bronson's persona.

As for directors, Bronson had hardly worked with the pick of the bunch. Michael Winner has a certain flair for making popular movies slightly more interesting, and Tom Gries, who directed *Breakout* and *Breakheart Pass,* has shown that with better material, like his earlier *Will Penny*, he could become an outstanding director. The rest were competent, efficient, hack technicians. That, of course, was why they had been chosen. The films had been built around Bronson, and his was the 'vision' that was imposed upon them; the directors were just there to position the cameras. The problem was that Bronson himself had no vision to impose, only his increasingly stereotyped image.

Don Siegel, it was hoped, would be different, and there was no chance of Lee Remick being 'presenced' off the screen by anyone. In some respects the hopes were fulfilled; *Telefon* did prove to be the best movie Bronson had made in a long time. Not that it faced much competition.

The plot-line might have been dreamt up by the authors of *The White Buffalo* on their day off. It transpires that in the bad old days (the cold war 1950s) the Soviet enemy has used hypnosis to programme a number of ordinary, unwitting Americans to undertake sabotage missions on receipt of a coded telephone message. Now, in the good old days of detente, a madman (Donald Pleasance) is going from town to town activating these saboteurs, and the Soviets send top agent Borzov (Bronson) to stop him. He meets up with fellow KGB agent Barbara (Lee Remick)—she is naturally a double—and between them they struggle to make the world safe for CIA-KGB partnership. And they fall in love.

Some critics were less than impressed. One review began 'this dismal attempt', another noted 'the relentless banality of Hyam's and Silliphant's script'. *Telefon* is certainly not a good movie by Siegel's earlier standards. The plot is far-fetched and, even worse, full of gaping logical holes. The

level of 'truth' sustained by the characters and the
world they inhabit is not noticeably high.

What saves the film is the interaction between
the two principals. As *Films and Filming* put it:
'Bronson and Remick play beautifully together,
against all expectation.' Against all their expectations anyway. In *Telefon*, Bronson hinted at what
he could have achieved with stronger feminine
and directorial presences in his films.

What goes up must come down

THE TROUBLE WITH *Telefon* was that it didn't make money. Whether this lack of commercial success reflected the film itself, or on those which had gone before it, was hard to tell at the time, but the even more disastrous showing of *Love and Bullets* pointed to the latter reason. This film exemplified everything that was wrong with Bronson's post-*Death Wish* movies.

Once again Jill Ireland took the female lead, once again Bronson held his lips tightly together, hooded his eyes at the right moments, and pointed his pistol well. The script could have been written on the back of a beer mat—something along the lines of 'pick out two photogenic locations (Arizona and Switzerland?), shoot chase scenes, betrayal scenes and violent scenes in each, and then shuffle them into some sort of coherent order'. It was commercial cinema at its mindless worst, a fact apparently appreciated by Rod Steiger, who played his Mafia leader so far over the top as to approach farce. *Love and Bullets* was not only a waste of his and

Bronson's talents, but also a commercial disaster, not even gaining a general release in the States.

By this time (1977-8) it was apparent to both Bronson and the industry that his star was on the wane. In America, particularly, his name was no longer enough to fill the cinemas; the formula had worked itself out. He would henceforth have to work with other top stars, with better directors and with more imaginative screenplays.

Bronson himself seemed both resentful and resigned. 'Nobody stays on top for ever,' he said in 1979. 'Nobody! It's impossible.' But he didn't like the falling sensation. 'I have a million people on my back, and one thing is for sure: when you're not at the pinnacle you find out fast who's your friend and who isn't.' There was a lot of defiance in the air. 'I used to be uncomfortable because people said I was a star and not an actor; well, when you have enough money, labels don't matter much. Anyway you get a different audience that goes to see my flicks than goes to see, say, Robert Redford's or especially someone like Peter Sellers or Olivier. I'm not trying to be anything I'm not. I tell people to accept me or reject me—just don't try and change me.'

Meanwhile, back in Hollywood, one of the ideas-men must have been having an idea. The scene is imaginable:

FIRST IDEAS-MAN: I know, let's re-make *Casablanca*.
SECOND IDEAS-MAN: It can't be done.
FIRST: OK then, let's make a picture just like *Casablanca*, with the same sort of story —you know, exotic location, unre-

129

	quited love, Nazi villains—and call it something similar ... change a few letters ... how about *Cabo Blanco*?
SECOND:	Sounds good. What about stars? Who can play Humphrey Bogart?
FIRST:	Bronson had a try in *Breakout*. He looks tough enough. But we need a foreign woman to play Ingrid Bergman...
SECOND:	Dominique Sanda. And Jason Robards for the Nazi. He was great in *All The President's Men*.
FIRST:	Yes, yes, Now blanco means white, doesn't it? Well J. Lee Thompson did a great job with *The White Buffalo*...

It is in such a way, perhaps, that white elephants are born. Considering its likely genesis *Cabo Blanco* was not such a bad film, merely one which failed to get anywhere near the level of excellence displayed by its cinematic prototype. It wasn't the plot which turned *Casablanca* into a classic; it was the performances, the atmosphere—both exotic and claustrophobic—and, above all, the dialogue. *Cabo Blanco* failed on all three counts, particularly the last two. Bronson, on set, thought it a 'damned good movie. I think someday it's going to be a cult film, after it's a box office hit.' His judgment had rarely been worse. It might one day become a cult film—stranger things have happened—but it was light years away from being a box-office hit. Something else would be needed to restore Bronson's waning popularity.

The publicity release which accompanied his next film told it all. 'BORDERLINE' NOT YOUR AVERAGE CHARLES BRONSON FILM ran the headline. Unfortunately the synopsis attached, and the film itself, belied such claims. Though set amidst the topical problems of the US-Mexican border, though full of good intentions, *Borderline* was indeed no more and no less an animal than 'your average Charles Bronson film'.

But did it worry Bronson too much? By the end of the decade he was hardly itching to make movies. He was approaching sixty, quite an age for an actor who had always relied a great deal on physical movement. 'I'm not croaking out one flick after another now,' he said in 1979. 'Of course, I've got enough for the rest of my life and my kids' lives, but I'm a trouper, I like to get my hands dirty. Only I won't do it unless I'm fully satisfied about everything that's going on. Us legends tend to get picky in our twilight years.'

In one way *Death Hunt* would have made a fitting end to his long career. Three decades earlier he and Lee Marvin had made their film debuts in *U.S.S. Teakettle*; now here they were, two grizzled legends, chasing each other across Arctic Canada, pausing only to admire each other's skill and to lament the passing of older days. 'The future has arrived,' the arrogant young flier tells Marvin's mountie, minutes before plunging his plane into some very hard earth. The audience already has the message—Marvin having told the flier that 'if you're the future, I don't want to see it'. He seems to be playing a composite of all his roles, a hard, tough, world-weary, wise, drunken and craggy survivor with a heart of pickled gold.

Bronson too is cast as a composite legend. He's

hard and tough too, but he's not the sort to drink. He rarely speaks with his mouth; the eyes say all he has to tell: keep your distance. He needs no one, trusts no one, wants no one. Society is just a snare and a delusion, and he's learnt to live without it. He doesn't have a heart of gold, anymore than a wild animal would have one. Nature is not a sentimental business.

If *Death Hunt* had been made fifteen years earlier, with better dialogue, it might have been a great film. As it is, the familiarity of the actors detracts from their characters. It doesn't seem real. These aren't legendary people involved in a life-and-death drama, they're legendary actors making another movie.

Where do grizzled legends go? In *Death Hunt*, for the first time, Bronson looked and sounded his age. The 'presence' was still there, but it was no longer so physical; the sense of coiled power, waiting to explode into action, was gone. He would not be playing the likes of 'Harmonica' or Pardon Chato again.

Paul Kersey was another matter. A sequel to *Death Wish* had been on the cards for years, and in the summer of 1981 Bronson was stalking the streets once more with a gun in his pocket and murder in his heart. According to director Winner 'the story's fairly similar. Quite a few new angles, and times have changed a bit, but most sequels that are successful don't wander too far from the original.' The main change was a shift of location; this time round it would be Los Angeles, America's new crime capital, which

132

would feel the vigilante's displeasure. And, probably, flock to see the film. Before shooting had been completed, *Death Wish II* was vastly in profit on pre-sales.

Almost a century has passed since 'Walter' Bunchinsky set foot on Ellis Island in search of the American Dream. It seems somewhat ironic that his fifth son should now be earning million dollar fees for personifying journeys through the nightmare.

Bronson

BY THE FALL of 1981 Charles Bronson had appeared in seventy-two movies, a prodigious number by any standard. Many have now disappeared into the vaults or oblivion, many more have become simple TV fare, to be lifted from the shelves whenever a space in the programming demands. A few, a precious few, have deservedly become classics, and it is for these that Bronson will be remembered.

In 1975 he listed *Red Sun* and *Passager de la Pluie* as his personal favourites, and both are likely to figure high in any list of his best films. *Red Sun* was only one of several outstanding westerns he either appeared or starred in over a twenty-year period. *Once Upon A Time in the West*, a film brought close to perfection by his own performance, is undoubtedly a contender for the title of best western ever made.

Passager de la Pluie was a more interesting choice, in that its undeniable quality inadvertently highlights the lack of memorable films Bronson has made in modern dress. Of his starring vehicles only *Death Wish* stands out, and that, though set in present-day New York, was essentially a western. The 'contemporarisation' of the persona which shot him to superstardom was never successfully accomplished. In a way it couldn't be, because the essence of that persona was rooted in the past, in nature rather than society. Let loose in the modern world it became nothing more than a killing machine, differentiated only by the nature of the targets.

Looking back over his career to date it is hard to escape a sense of waste. The famous actor Charles Laughton once observed that Bronson 'has the strongest face in the business, and he is also one of its best actors'. For a man of such talents there have been too many bad films, too many nondescript films, too many similar films. Having proved in movies like *Machine Gun Kelly* and *Twinky* and *Breakout* that his range extended far beyond the stereotyped characters seen in 'The Stone Killer alias Chino Valdez alias Mr Majestyk *et al*', he carried on playing the stereotypes. It is a telling comment on Bronson's career that in two volumes of Paulene Kael's much-lauded film reviews, covering the years 1969-76, the years of his greatest popularity, not a single one of his films is featured. This may of course also be a telling comment on Paulene Kael, but that is the world Bronson has had to live and work in. If you don't keep the Paulene Kaels happy, at least some of the time, then you become a slave to the public, which these days means what the industry accountants ascribe to the public. Fashions change, or there'd be no money in fashion, and like everything else the past must move with the times.

Unlike some, Bronson has never forgotten that films are supposed to entertain, and for that he should be thanked. But the cinema, at its best, can be simultaneously entertaining, enlightening, uplifting, an interweaving of dream and reality. There is always room for good escapist garbage, but its creators can hardly expect to be revered for churning it out.

Bronson cannot be totally, or even greatly blamed for the disappointing quality of his output in the latter half of the 1970s. Anyone reaching superstardom after such a long and apparently fruitless slog must be forgiven for succumbing to the temptation to play it safe. And the American industry to which he returned in triumph was as disinclined to take risks as he was. The revitalisation of popular culture which occurred in the late 1960s and early 1970s was already beginning to live on its own momentum when the onset of the great recession further dampened the money-men's ardour for gambling on new ideas. Bronson might have gone on to greater things if he'd had a sound nose for good scripts and directors, but this was one talent which he definitely lacked.

Fortunately, the forgettable soon gets forgotten. We are left with the memorable, the stirring images from the great films: Kersey's anguish after claiming his first victim, O'Reilly lecturing the peasant children, Link's grief as Kuroda dies,

'Harmonica' appearing, as if by magic, from behind the departing train. The ancient race at war with the modern world. 'Just a man.' No more, no less.

Filmography

U.S.S. Teakettle (You're in the Navy Now) (1951)
Director: Henry Hathaway. Screenplay: Richard Murphy, from article by John W. Hazard. Producer: Fred Kohlmar. Stars: Gary Cooper, Jane Greer. Character: Wascylewski.

The People Against O'Hara (1951)
Director: John Sturges. Screenplay: John Monks Jr, from novel by Eleazar Lipsky. Producer: William H. Wright. Stars: Spencer Tracy, Pat O'Brien. Character: Angelo Korvac.

The Mob (Remember That Face) (1951)
Director: Robert Parrish. Screenplay: William Bowers, from story by Ferguson Findlay. Producer: Jerry Bresler. Stars: Broderick Crawford, Betty Buehler. Character: Jack.

Red Skies of Montana (1952)
Director: Joseph M. Newman. Screenplay: Harry Kleiner, from story by Art Cohn. Producer: Samuel G. Engel. Stars: Richard Widmark, Constance Smith, Jeffrey Hunter, Richard Boone. Character: Neff.

My Six Convicts (1952)
Director: Hugo Fregonese. Screenplay: Michael Blankfort, from novel by Donald Powell Wilson. Producer: Stanley Kramer. Stars: Millard Mitchell, Gilbert Roland. Character: 'convict'.

The Marrying Kind (1952)
Director: George Cukor. Screenplay: Ruth Gordon and Garson Kanin. Producer: Bert Granet. Stars: Judy Holliday, Aldo Ray. Character: Eddie.

Diplomatic Courier (1952)
Director: Henry Hathaway. Screenplay: Casey Robinson and Liam O'Brien, from Peter Cheyney's novel *Sinister Errand*. Producer: Casey Robinson. Stars: Tyrone Power, Patricia Neal. Character: 'bit'.

Bloodhounds of Broadway (1952)
Director: Harmon Jones. Screenplay: Sy Gomberg. Producer: George Jessel. Stars: Mitzi Gaynor, Scott Brady. Character: Pittsburgh Philo.

The Clown (1953)
Director: Robert Z. Leonard. Screenplay: Martin Rackin. Producer: William H. Wright. Star: Red Skelton. Character: Eddie.

House of Wax (1953)
Director: André de Toth. Screenplay: Crane Wilbur, from Charles Belden's play. Producer: Bryan Foy. Star: Vincent Price. Character: Igor.

Miss Sadie Thompson (1954)
Director: Curtis Bernhardt. Screenplay: Harry Klein, from Somerset Maugham's play *Rain*. Producer: Jerry Wald. Stars: Rita Hayworth, José Ferrer, Aldo Ray. Character: Edwards.

Crime Wave (The City is Dark) (1954)
Director: André de Toth. Screenplay: Crane Wilbur. Producer: Bryan Foy. Stars: Gene Nelson, Phyllis Kirk, Sterling Hayden. Character: Ben Hastings.

Tennessee Champ (1954)
Director: Fred M. Wilcox. Screenplay: Art Cohn, from stories by Eustace Cockrell. Producer: Sol Baer Fielding. Stars: Shelley Winters, Keenan Wynn. Character: Sixty Jubel.

Riding Shotgun (1954)
Director: André de Toth. Screenplay: Tom Blackburn, from story by Kenneth Perkins. Producer: Ted Sherdeman. Star: Randolph Scott. Character: Pinto.

Apache (1954)
Director: Robert Aldrich. Screenplay: James E. Webb, from novel by Paul I. Wellman. Producer: Harold Hecht. Stars: Burt Lancaster, Jean Peters. Character: Hondo.

Drum Beat (1954)
Director: Delmer Daves. Screenplay: Delmer Daves. Producer: Delmer Daves. Star: Alan Ladd. Character: Captain Jack.

Vera Cruz (1954)
Director: Robert Aldrich. Screenplay: Roland Kibbee and James R. Webb, from story by Borden Chase. Producer: James Hill. Stars: Gary Cooper, Burt Lancaster. Character: Pittsburgh.

Big House U.S.A. (1955)
Director: Howard W. Koch. Screenplay: John C. Higgins. Producer: Aubrey Schenck. Stars: Broderick Crawford, Ralph Meeker. Character: Benny Kelly.

Target Zero (1955)
Director: Harmon Jones. Screenplay: Sam Rolfe, from story by James Warner Bellah. Producer: David Weisbart. Co-stars: Richard Conte, Peggie Castle. Character: Sgt. Vince Gaspari.

Jubal (1956)
Director: Delmer Daves. Screenplay: Russell S. Hughes and Delmer Daves, from Paul I. Wellman's novel. Producer: William Fadiman. Stars: Glenn Ford, Ernest Borgnine, Rod Steiger, Valerie French, Felicia Farr. Character: Reb Haislipp.

Run of the Arrow (1957)
Director: Samuel Fuller. Screenplay: Samuel Fuller. Producer: Samuel Fuller. Stars: Rod Steiger, Sarita Montiel. Character: Blue Buffalo.

Gang War (1958)
Director: Gene Fowler Jr. Screenplay: Louis Vittes, from Ovid Demaris' novel *The Hoods Take Over*. Producer: Harold E. Knox. Co-stars: Kent Taylor, Jennifer Holden. Character: Alan Avery.

Showdown at Boot Hill (1958)
Director: Gene Fowler Jr. Screenplay: Louis
Vittes. Producer: Harold E. Knox. Co-stars:
Robert Hutton, John Carradine, Carole
Mathews. Character: Luke Welsh.

When Hell Broke Loose (1958)
Director: Kenneth G. Crane. Screenplay: Oscar
Brodney, from articles by Ib Melchoir.
Producers: Oscar Brodney and Sal Dolgin. Co-
stars: Violet Rensing, Richard Jaeckel. Character:
Steve Boland.

Machine Gun Kelly (1958)
Director: Roger Corman. Screenplay: R. Wright
Campbell. Producer: Roger Corman. Co-star:
Susan Cabot. Character: Machine Gun Kelly.

Ten North Frederick (1958)
Director: Philip Dunne. Screenplay: Philip
Dunne. Producer: Charles Bracket. Stars: Gary
Cooper, Suzy Parker, Geraldine Fitzgerald, Diane
Varsi. Character: 'it'.

Never So Few (1959)
Director: John Sturges. Screenplay: Millard
Kaufman, from novel by Tom T. Chamales.
Producer: Edmund Grainger. Stars: Frank
Sinatra, Gina Lollobrigida, Peter Lawford, Steve
McQueen. Character: Sgt. Danforth.

The Magnificent Seven (1960)
Director: John Sturges. Screenplay: William
Roberts, from Akiro Kurosawa's film *The Seven
Samurai*. Producer: John Sturges. Co-stars: Yul

Brynner, Eli Wallach, Steve McQueen, Horst Buchholz, James Coburn, Robert Vaughn. Character: O'Reilly.

Master of the World (1961)
Director: William Witney. Screenplay: Richard Matheson, from two novels by Jules Verne. Producer: James H. Nicholson. Co-stars: Vincent Price, Henry Hull, Mary Webster. Character: Strock.

A Thunder of Drums (1961)
Director: Joseph M. Newman. Screenplay: James Warner Bellah. Producer: Robert J. Enders. Stars: Richard Boone, George Hamilton, Luana Patten. Character: Trooper Hanna.

X-15 (1961)
Director: Richard Donner. Screenplay: Tony Lazzarino and James Warner Bellah, from former's story. Producers: Henry Sanicola and Tony Lazzarino. Co-stars: David McLean, Ralph Taeger. Character: Lt.Col. Lee Brandon.

This Rugged Land (1962)
Director: Arthur Hiller. (Spin-off from TV series *Empire*.) Co-stars: Richard Egan, Ryan O'Neal. Character: Paul Moreno.

Kid Galahad (1962)
Director: Phil Karlson. Screenplay: William Fay, from story by Francis Wallace. Producer: David Weisbart. Star: Elvis Presley. Character: Lew Nyack.

The Great Escape (1963)
Director: John Sturges. Screenplay: James Clavell and W. R. Burnett, from Paul Brickhill's novel. Producer: John Sturges. Co-stars: Steve McQueen, Richard Attenborough, James Garner, James Coburn, David McCallum, Donald Pleasance, James Donald. Character: Danny 'Tunnel King'.

Four for Texas (1963)
Director: Robert Aldrich. Screenplay: Teddi Sherman and Robert Aldrich. Producer: Robert Aldrich. Co-stars: Frank Sinatra, Dean Martin, Ursula Andress, Anita Ekberg. Character: Matson.

Guns of Diablo (1964)
Director: Boris Sagal. (Spin-off from TV series *The Travels of Jamie McPheeters*.) Co-stars: Susan Oliver, Kurt Russell. Character: Linc Murdoch.

The Sandpiper (1965)
Director: Vincente Minelli. Screenplay: Dalton Trumbo and Michael Wilson, from story by Martin Ransohoff. Producer: Martin Ransohoff. Stars: Elizabeth Taylor, Richard Burton, Eva Marie Saint. Character: Cos.

The Battle of the Bulge (1965)
Director: Ken Annakin. Screenplay: Philip Yordan, Milton Sperling and John Melson. Producers: Milton Sperling and Philip Yordan. Co-stars: Henry Fonda, Robert Shaw, Robert Ryan, Dana Andrews, George Montgomery, Ty Hardin, Pier Angeli, Telly Savalas. Character: Wolenski.

This Property is Condemned (1966)
Director: Sydney Pollack. Screenplay: Francis
Ford Coppola, Fred Coe and Edith Sommer.
Producer: John Houseman. Stars: Natalie Wood,
Robert Redford. Character: J. J. Nichols.

The Dirty Dozen (1967)
Director: Robert Aldrich. Screenplay: Nunnally
Johnson and Lukas Heller, from novel by E. M.
Nathanson. Producer: Kenneth Hyman. Co-
stars: Lee Marvin, Ernest Borgnine, Jim Brown,
John Cassavetes, Richard Jaeckel. Character:
Joseph Wladislaw.

Guns for San Sebastian (1967)
Director: Henri Verneuil. Screenplay (English):
James R. Webb, from William Barby Faherty's
novel *A Wall for San Sebastian*. Producer: Jacques
Bar. Co-stars: Anthony Quinn, Anjanette Comer.
Character: Teclo.

Villa Rides (1968)
Director: Buzz Kulik. Screenplay: Robert Towne
and Sam Peckinpah, from William Douglas
Lansford's novel *Pancho Villa*. Producer: Ted
Richmond. Co-stars: Yul Brynner, Robert
Mitchum. Character: Fierro.

Adieu l'Ami (1968)
Director: Jean Herman. Screenplay: Jean
Herman and Sebastian Japrisot. Producer: Jean
Herman. Co-star: Alain Delon. Character: Franz
Propp.

Once Upon A Time in the West (1969)
Director: Sergio Leone. Screenplay: Sergio
Leone and Sergio Dnati, from story by Dario
Argento, Sergio Leone and Bernardo Bertolucci.
Producer: Fulvio Morsella. Co-stars: Henry
Fonda, Claudia Cardinale, Jason Robards.
Character: 'Harmonica'.

Passager de la Pluie (Rider on the Rain) (1969)
Director: Rene Clement. Screenplay: Sebastian
Japrisot. Producer: Serge Silberman. Co-star:
Marlene Joubert. Character: Dobbs.

Twinky (Lola) (1970)
Director: Richard Donner. Screenplay: Norman
Thaddeus Vane. Producer: Clive Sharp. Co-star:
Susan George. Character: Scott Wardman.

You Can't Win'em All (1970)
Director: Peter Collison. Screenplay: Leo V.
Gordon. Producer: Gene Corman. Co-stars:
Tony Curtis, Michele Mercier. Character: Josh
Corey.

Citta Violenta (Violent City) (1970)
Director: Serge Sollima. Screenplay: Sauro
Scavolini, Gianfranco Calligarich, Lina Wert-
muller and Serge Sollima, from story by Dino
Maiuri and Massimo De Rita. Producers: Harry
Colombo, George Papi. Co-stars: Jill Ireland,
Michael Constantin, Telly Savalas. Character:
Jeff.

Cold Sweat (1970)
Director: Terence Young. Screenplay: Shimon Wincelberg and Albert Simonin, from Richard Matheson's novel *Ride the Nightmare*. Producer: Robert Dorfmann. Co-stars: Liv Ullman, James Mason, Jill Ireland. Character: Joe Martin.

Someone Behind the Door (1971)
Director: Nicolas Gessner. Screenplay: Jacques Robert, Marc Behm, Nicolas Gessner and Lorenzo Ventavoli, from novel by Jacques Robert. Producer: Raymond Danon. Co-stars: Anthony Perkins, Jill Ireland. Character: Amnesiac.

Red Sun (1971)
Director: Terence Young. Screenplay: Laird Koenig, Denne Bart Petitclerc, William Roberts and Lawrence Roman, from story by Laird Koenig. Producer: Ted Richmond. Co-stars: Toshiro Mifune, Alain Delon, Ursula Andress, Capucine. Character: Link.

Chato's Land (1972)
Director: Michael Winner. Screenplay: Gerald Wilson. Producer: Michael Winner. Co-stars: Jack Palance, Richard Basehart, James Whitmore. Character: Pardon Chato.

The Valachi Papers (1972)
Director: Terence Young. Screenplay: Stephen Geller, from *The Valachi Papers* by Peter Maas. Producer: Dino de Laurentiis. Co-stars: Joseph Wiseman, Jill Ireland. Character: Joseph Valachi.

The Mechanic (Killer of Killers) (1972)
Director: Michael Winner. Screenplay: Lewis
John Carlino. Producers: Irwin Winkler and
Robert Chartoff. Co-stars: Jan Michael Vincent,
Keenan Wynn, Jill Ireland. Character: Arthur
Bishop.

The Valdez Horses (Valdez the Halfbreed) (1973)
Director: John Sturges. Screenplay: Dino Maiuri,
Massimo De Rita and Clair Huffaker, from Lee
Hoffman's novel *The Valdez Horses*. Producer:
Duilio Coletti. Co-stars: Jill Ireland, Vincent Van
Patten, Marcel Bozzuffi. Character: Chino
Valdez.

The Stone Killer (1973)
Director: Michael Winner. Screenplay: Gerald
Wilson, from John Gardner's novel *A Complete
State of Death*. Producer: Michael Winner. Co-
star: Martin Balsam. Character: Detective Lou
Torrey.

Mr Majestyk (1974)
Director: Richard Fleischer. Screenplay: Elmore
Leonard. Producer: Walter Mirisch. Co-stars: Al
Lettieri, Linda Crystal, Lee Purcell. Character:
Vince Majestyk.

Death Wish (1974)
Director: Michael Winner. Screenplay: Wendell
Mayes, from novel by Brian Garfield. Producers:
Hal Landers and Bobby Roberts. Co-stars:
Vincent Gardenia, Steven Keats, Hope Lange,
Stuart Margolin. Character: Paul Kersey.

Breakout (1975)
Director: Tom Gries. Screenplay: Howard B. Kreitsek, Marc Norman and Elliot Baker, from novel by Warren Hinckle, William Turner and Eliot Asinof. Producers: Irwin Winkler and Robert Chartoff. Co-stars: Robert Duvall, Jill Ireland, John Huston, Randy Quaid, Sheree North. Character: Nick Colton.

Hard Times (The Streetfighter) (1975)
Director: Walter Hill. Screenplay: Walter Hill. Producer: Lawrence Gordon. Co-stars: James Coburn, Jill Ireland, Strother Martin. Character: Chaney.

Breakheart Pass (1975)
Director: Tom Gries. Screenplay: Alistair MacLean from own novel. Producer: Jerry Gershwin. Co-stars: Ben Johnson, Jill Ireland, Richard Crenna. Character: John Deakin.

From Noon Til Three (1976)
Director: Frank D. Gilroy. Screenplay: Frank D. Gilroy from own novel. Producers: M. J. Frankovich and William Self. Co-star: Jill Ireland. Character: Dorsey.

St Ives (1976)
Director: J. Lee Thompson. Screenplay: Barry Beckerman, from Oliver Bleeck's novel *The Procane Chronicle*. Producers: Pancho Kohner and Stanley Carter. Co-stars: John Houseman, Jacqueline Bisset. Character: Raymond St Ives.

Raid on Entebbe (1977)
Director: Irvin Kershner. Screenplay: Barry Beckerman. Producers: Edgar J. Sherick and Daniel H. Blatt. Co-stars: Peter Finch, Yaphet Kotto, Jack Warden, Martin Balsam, Horst Buchholz. Character: Brig-Gen. Dan Shomron.

The White Buffalo (1977)
Director: J. Lee Thompson. Screenplay: Richard Sale, from own novel. Producer: Pancho Kohner. Co-stars: Jack Warden, Will Sampson, Kim Novak, Clint Walker. Character: Wild Bill Hickok, alias James Otis.

Telefon (1977)
Director: Don Siegel. Screenplay: Peter Hyams and Stirling Silliphant. Producer: James B. Harris. Co-stars: Lee Remick, Donald Pleasance, Tyne Daly, Alan Badel. Character: Grigori Borzov.

Love and Bullets (1978)
Director: Stuart Rosenberg. Screenplay: Wendell Mayes and John Melson. Producer: Pancho Kohner. Co-stars: Jill Ireland, Rod Steiger. Character: Charlie Congers.

Cabo Blanco (1979)
Director: J. Lee Thompson. Screenplay: Milt Gelman. Producers: Lance Hool and Paul A. Joseph. Co-stars: Dominique Sanda, Jason Robards, Ferando Rey, Simon McCorkindale, Camilla Sparv. Character: Giff Hoyt.

Borderline (1980)
Director: Jerrold Freedman. Screenplay: Jerrold Freedman and Steve Kline. Producer: James Nelson. Co-stars: Bruno Kirby, Bert Remsen, Michael Lerner. Character: Jeb Maynard.

Death Hunt (1981)
Director: Peter Hunt. Screenplay: Michael Grais and Mark Victor. Producer: Murray Shostak. Co-stars: Lee Marvin, Ed Lauter, Carl Weathers. Character: Albert Johnson.

Death Wish II (1981)
Director: Michael Winner. Producers: Hal Landers and Bobby Roberts. Co-stars: Jill Ireland, Vincent Gardenia. Character: Paul Kersey.

Index

153

154